ROCK & ROLL

TED GREENWALD

ROCK&ROLL

THE MUSIC, MUSICIANS, AND THE MANIA

MALLARD
PRESS

A FRIEDMAN GROUP BOOK

Published by MALLARD PRESS
An Imprint of BDD Promotional Book Company, Inc.
666 Fifth Avenue
New York, N.Y. 10103

Mallard Press and the accompanying duck logo are registered
trademarks of the BDD Promotional Book Company, Inc.
Registered in the U.S. Patent and Trademark Office.

ISBN 0-7924-5765-X

ROCK AND ROLL
The Music, Musicians, and the Mania
was prepared and produced by
Michael Friedman Publishing Group, Inc.
15 West 26th Street
New York, New York 10010

Editor: Elizabeth Viscott Sullivan
Art Director: Jeff Batzli
Designer: Charles Donahue
Photography Editor: Daniella Jo Nilva

Typeset by Classic Type, Inc.
Color separations by Rainbow Graphic Arts Co.
Printed and bound in Hong Kong by Leefung-Asco Printers Ltd.

Acknowledgements

A book of this scope would have been impossible
without the generous help of a number of authori-
ties on various aspects of rock and roll. Valuable
perspectives were contributed by Gary Arnet, Adam
Bresnick, Fraser Brown, Michael Macrone, George
Makari, Steph Paynes, Robert J. Seidenberg, and
Jay-Gould Stuckey. Thanks are also due to the many
record companies that provided information about
their recording artists, including A&M, Atlantic,
Capitol, Columbia, Elektra, Epic, Geffen, MCA,
Sire, Virgin, Warner Bros., and Wax Trax. In addition, a number of organizations provided their
expertise, including MTV, the National Academy of
Recording Arts and Sciences (NARAS), and the
Rock and Roll Hall of Fame and Museum. The
author offers extra-special thanks to Merrill Gruver
for her enthusiasm, thoughtful criticism, and
unflagging support.

Contents

IT'S ONLY ROCK AND ROLL

Pete Townshend once said that if he didn't go onstage, his fans would have nothing to live for. Lou Reed confirms the notion, insisting that rock and roll kept him alive during his teenage years. Bruce Springsteen calls the music "the great motivator." Indeed, rock and roll motivates people throughout the world to buy records, make their own music, and pursue dreams that aren't related to music at all.

It's odd that rock and roll, a branch of popular music based on the glories and tortures of adolescence, can mean so much to so many people. But it does, as it has for nearly four decades, and it will continue to do so as surely as the snare's crack follows the kick drum.

To many, rock and roll is a soundtrack for the drama of daily life. Rock and roll fuses the mythic quality of our strivings and the bittersweet flavor of our deepest desires with the cold, hard reality of life itself. It offers an emotional mooring, a way of locating ourselves amidst the barrage of images and experiences that is life on the brink of the twenty-first century. In the great tradition of mystic artistry, rock and roll dares to speak the unspeakable, even when the result is no more articulate than Little Richard's transcendent lyric, "awop-bop-aloo-bop, alop-bam-boom."

But is it art? Well, yes and no. For the most part, it's business. Aspiring bands are often as interested in stardom as they are in music—and that includes Chuck Berry, the Beatles, Hendrix, Sly, Springsteen, the Sex Pistols, and Public Enemy. On the other hand, even the most dedicated minimalist couldn't wring as much formal elegance, not to mention emotional juice, out of the phrase "I wanna be your man" as the Beatles did in 1964. If rock and roll isn't art, then neither is the rest of contemporary culture, from books to films to architecture. It all exists within the same commercial media milieu.

The false distinction between "commercial" and "noncommercial" music becomes clear when a fringe subgenre suddenly is incorporated into mainstream tastes, as happened during the late seventies when rather effete progressive rock groups began filling stadiums. Their music, originally aimed at a cult audience, gradually found an ever-widening market niche. As the bands sought to satisfy that niche, it became broader still. When such a niche becomes broad enough to include tens of millions of people across national and ethnic boundaries, it crosses the vague line between rock and roll and something more properly called "pop."

Pop is, in a sense, anything that sells massively, gigantically, hugely big. In order to appeal to a wide audience, pop music tends to smooth its rough edges, cover its pitted surfaces, and decorate its spare furnishings. Rock and roll, on the other hand, values rough edges as hallmarks of spontaneity, pitted surfaces as evidence of personal authenticity, and spare furnishings as an expression of humility and solidarity with ordinary folk. Rock and roll has always had an antisocial streak, celebrating (or at least leaving open the possibility of) defiance of authority, illicit sex, and even violence. But insofar as rock and roll aspires to widespread popularity—which it always has, with a brief respite during the punk rock era—it partakes of a pop aesthetic.

Therefore, no purely "pop" category appears in the rock and roll family tree on page 9. Because the rock and roll audience is a mass phenomenon, the music rests on a bedrock of pop that may exert more or less influence, but never disappears entirely. The family tree attempts to trace the lines of influence that constitute rock and roll history, from the germinal energy of the blues and country to the present cornucopia of subgenres.

The tree's structure makes it possible to trace the country influence in Bruce Springsteen's music from rockabilly through the British Invasion and folk rock to the "post-Dylan American Heroic"

tradition. Some lines are stronger than others. On the other hand, many of the less essential ones, such as the feedback between disco and techno-pop and the complex connections between metal, glitter, and punk, have been omitted in order to avoid clutter.

Stuffing works of art into neat little cubbyholes is likely to please neither fans nor artists, who hold emotional investments in the uniqueness and originality that infuse the best rock and roll. And, it must be said, the most popular artists, including Chicago, Elton John, and Joni Mitchell, tend to defy categorization even as they help to define categories into which other artists fall. Nonetheless, the music of the past does exert an influence on the music of the present, as cover versions and artist interviews attest. Perhaps the best way to consider the lines and categories on the tree is as answers to the question: Whose songs did a given band most likely play in their garage days, before they started writing their own material?

Any subgenre in the tree can comprise a number of divisions and variations, only the most significant of which appear as categories in their own right—for instance, pop metal as an aspect of metal. Most rock and roll substyles have distinct American and British schools (punk is a good example), as well as divisions that lean more heavily on African or European backgrounds. Most include a pop extreme (say, folk rockers Sonny and Cher) and an arty extreme (say, folk rocker Bob Dylan).

It's also important to recognize that the subgenres in the tree don't necessarily die out after their inception. A subgenre as old as blue-eyed soul continues in the nineties with representatives such as Hall & Oates; although the duo is obviously influenced by current styles as well, the Righteous Brothers remain the fundamental reference point for their music.

Dates on the tree represent the seminal recording in a given subgenre (see the list on page 8). This can lead to some distortions, since a musical movement may exist for years before anyone has enough faith in its marketability to release a record. Still, records are virtually the sole means by which

a new subgenre becomes influential; they also account for influences that may be separated by many years—for example, the late-sixties releases by the Velvet Underground that set the tone for punk rock a decade later. Records are the only tangible remains of many extinct forms of rock and roll, and for the purpose of this book, record releases are regarded as crucial events in rock history.

The family tree may be viewed as a relatively inclusive, if idiosyncratic, definition of rock and roll in all of its musical manifestations. But rock and roll is, of course, more than music. It is clothing and hair styles, social criticism, a manifestation of sociological forces, and an agent of change, not to mention a body of lyrics that can be interpreted in a number of ways. Rock and roll is a grand experiment in free speech and cultural interchange, in global marketing and the mass production of art.

In the nineties, the music is shaping up as a medium through which disparate segments of society can mingle publicly, forging cultural alliances that may serve to unite traditionally separate factions even as the music itself fragments along lines drawn ever more finely. "Bring on the Noise," a collaboration among metalheads Anthrax and black-power propagandists Public Enemy, suggests that the lines of influence charted by this book are becoming hopelessly tangled, and perhaps are well on their way toward dissolving entirely.

Above all, over nearly four decades, rock and roll has remained something that people can believe in. It is tried and true, direct, honest, and elemental, a source of identity and community that is continually self-renewing. In the words of Neil Young, there's more to the picture than meets the eye.

Hey hey, my my.

Center: Since its appropriation by charismatic rockers during the late 1950s, the electric guitar, with its extreme loudness and streamlined shape, has come to symbolize the rebellious, erotic power of rock and roll.

Rock and Roll Family Tree

The rock and roll family tree attempts to trace the lines of influence that constitute rock and roll history. The dates mark the first identifiable appearance of a new subgenre in the form of a record release. (The artists and titles of those records are listed here.)

A given subgenre doesn't necessarily die out after its inception; many of the earliest are still going strong in the nineties. Nor does an artist's identification with a given subgenre necessarily limit his or her activity to that classification; artists such as David Bowie metamorphose with disarming ease, remaining in any camp for no more than a few years, while others, like Joni Mitchell, produce an art so distinctive that it both defines and transcends its own category. Furthermore, within a given subgenre there are likely to be divisions, such as an artsy branch and a pop branch, or American or British schools.

Some entries in the tree, notably house and industrial, are still too new and/or too obscure to identify their dates of inception or prototypical recordings. Only time will tell whether they are evolutionary blind alleys or pathways to the rock and roll future.

Crooners: "I've Got the Girl" by Bing Crosby & Gus Arnheim Band, 1926

Jump: "Gee, But You're Swell" by Louis Jordan, 1937

Chicago Blues: "Gypsy Woman"/"Little Anna Mae" by Muddy Waters, 1947

Rhythm & Gospel: "Have Mercy, Baby" by the Dominoes, 1952

Rockabilly: "That's All Right"/"Blue Moon of Kentucky" by Elvis Presley, 1954

Classic Rock and Roll: "Maybelline" by Chuck Berry, 1955

Proto-Soul: "Please, Please, Please" by James Brown, 1956

Ska: "Little Honey" by Prince Buster, 1956

Teen Idols: First broadcast of *American Bandstand,* 1957

Girl Groups: "Maybe" by the Chantels, 1958

Motown: "Way Over There" by Smokey Robinson & the Miracles, 1960

Memphis Soul: "Just Out of Reach" by Solomon Burke, 1961

Surf Rock: "Surfin'" by the Beach Boys, 1961

Blue-Eyed Soul: *The Righteous Brothers,* 1963

London Blues Revival: *Live at Klook's Kleek* by John Mayall's Bluesbreakers, 1963

British Invasion: "I Want to Hold Your Hand" by the Beatles, 1964

American Defense: "Come a Little Bit Closer" by Jay & the Americans, 1964

U.S. Folk Rock: "Mr. Tambourine Man" by the Byrds, 1965

Funk: "Papa's Got a Brand New Bag" by James Brown, 1965

Blues Rock: *Fresh Cream,* 1966

Psychedelia: *Jefferson Airplane Takes Off,* 1966

Rock Steady: "Rock Steady" by Anton Ellis, 1966

Arty Primitivism: *The Velvet Underground & Nico,* 1967

U.K. Folk Rock: *Fairport Convention,* 1968

Bubblegum: First broadcast of *The Archies,* 1968

Hard Rock: "Born to be Wild" by Steppenwolf, 1968

Country Rock: *Sweetheart of the Rodeo,* by the Byrds, 1968

Philly Soul: "Lost" by Jerry Butler, 1968

Progressive Rock: *The Thoughts of Emerlist Davjack* by the Nice, 1968

Reggae: "Do the Reggay" by Toots & the Maytals, 1969

Glitter Rock: *Pretties for You* by Alice Cooper, 1969

Southern Boogie: *The Allman Brothers Band,* 1969

Jazz Influences: *Bitches Brew* by Miles Davis, 1969

Confessional Singer/Songwriters: *James Taylor,* 1969

Pop-Rock Craftsmanship: *Empty Sky* by Elton John, 1969

L.A. Pop Rock: *Hand Sown, Home Grown* by Linda Ronstadt, 1969

Heavy Metal: *Black Sabbath,* 1970

Technopop/Technodance: *Kraftwerk,* 1971

Pop Metal: *Aerosmith,* 1973

Post-Dylan American Heroic: *Greetings From Asbury Park, N.J.* by Bruce Springsteen, 1973

Disco: "Do the Hustle" by Van McCoy, 1975

Hard Pop: *Boston,* 1976

Punk: *Ramones,* 1976

New Wave: *Blondie,* 1977

Postpunk: *Public Image Ltd.,* 1978

Two-Tone: *Specials,* 1979

Rap: "Christmas Rappin'" by Kurtis Blow, 1979

New Romantics and Pop Reactionaries: *Duran Duran,* 1980

Hardcore: *Damaged* by Black Flag, 1981

Post New Wave: "Radio Free Europe"/"Sitting Still" by R.E.M., 1982

Disco Revisionism: *Madonna,* 1983

Funk Metal: *Red Hot Chili Peppers,* 1984

Industrial: c. 1985

Speed Metal: *Master of Puppets* by Metallica, 1986

Retro Metal: *Appetite for Destruction* by Guns N' Roses, 1987

House: c. 1988

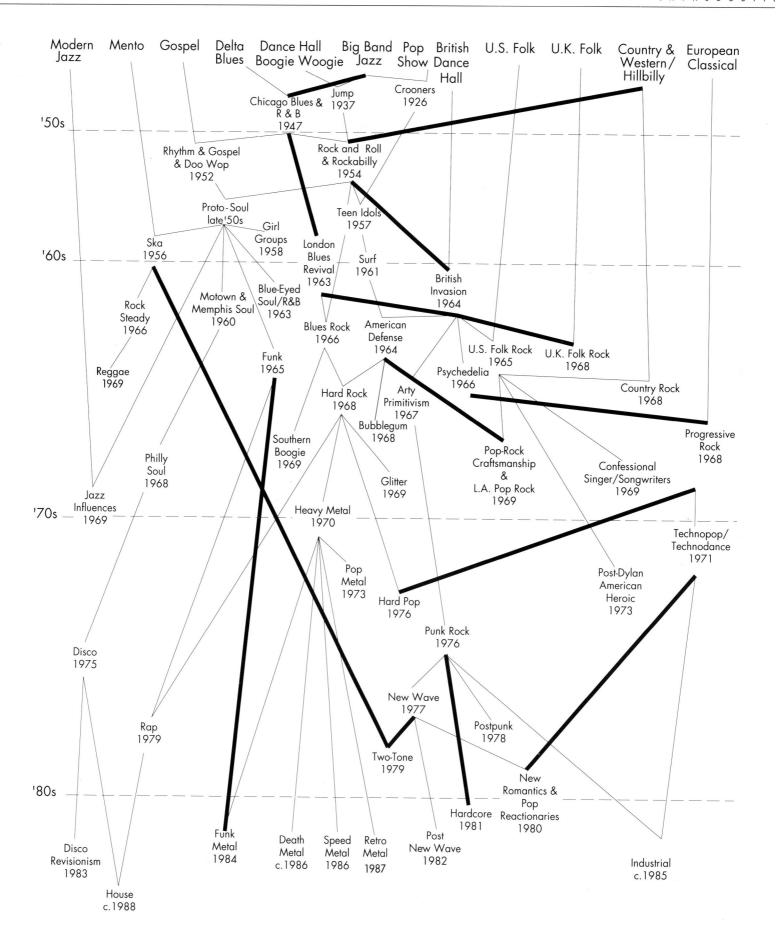

Modern Jazz

Mento

Gospel

Delta Blues

Dance Hall Boogie Woogie

Big Band Jazz

Pop Show

British Dance Hall

U.S. Folk

U.K. Folk

Country & Western / Hillbilly

European Classical

Chicago Blues & R & B 1947

Jump 1937

Crooners 1926

'50s

Rhythm & Gospel & Doo Wop 1952

Rock and Roll & Rockabilly 1954

Proto-Soul late '50s

Girl Groups 1958

London Blues Revival 1963

Teen Idols 1957

Ska 1956

'60s

Surf 1961

British Invasion 1964

Rock Steady 1966

Motown & Memphis Soul 1960

Blue-Eyed Soul/R&B 1963

Blues Rock 1966

American Defense 1964

U.S. Folk Rock 1965

U.K. Folk Rock 1968

Reggae 1969

Funk 1965

Hard Rock 1968

Arty Primitivism 1967

Psychedelia 1966

Country Rock 1968

Philly Soul 1968

Southern Boogie 1969

Bubblegum 1968

Pop-Rock Craftsmanship & L.A. Pop Rock 1969

Confessional Singer/Songwriters 1969

Progressive Rock 1968

Jazz Influences 1969

Glitter 1969

'70s

Heavy Metal 1970

Technopop/ Technodance 1971

Pop Metal 1973

Hard Pop 1976

Post-Dylan American Heroic 1973

Disco 1975

Punk Rock 1976

Rap 1979

New Wave 1977

Postpunk 1978

Two-Tone 1979

New Romantics & Pop Reactionaries 1980

'80s

Disco Revisionism 1983

Funk Metal 1984

Death Metal c.1986

Speed Metal 1986

Retro Metal 1987

Post New Wave 1982

Hardcore 1981

Industrial c.1985

House c.1988

Chapter One

The Foundation

SHAKE, RATTLE, AND ROLL:

RHYTHM AND BLUES AND THE BIRTH OF ROCK AND ROLL

In the history of the United States of America, the year 1954 doesn't particularly stand out. But against a backdrop of business-as-usual America, forces were converging that would erupt into what amounted to—in its impact on the culture of the nation and, indeed, on that of the world—a second American Revolution. The year 1954 served as midwife for the birth of rock and roll.

In politics, reactionary paranoia was the order of the day; that year, the American Communist Party was put out of business by Presidential decree. McCarthyite blacklisting kept entertainers deemed subversive out of the public eye, making today's arguments about record stickering and the proper use of federal arts funding sound wearily familiar. In 1954, good old American technological know-how was churning out whiz-bang new gadgets by the dozens, among them the color television, the transistor radio, and the atomic-powered submarine. Meanwhile, media stars like Marilyn Monroe and Joe DiMaggio entertained the masses via celebrity weddings on the order of Madonna and Sean Penn.

During the previous year, the recording industry had offered up such tame hits as "How Much is That Doggie in the Window?" by Patti Page and bland fare like Percy Faith's "Song From *Moulin Rouge.*" The marketing mavens of Madison Avenue had only recently recognized ethnic minorities as a viable segment of the population, and the undeniable moral force of the civil rights movement would soon make one of them—black America—ripe for a mainstream crossover. In 1954, the music of African-Americans, dubbed by the recording industry rhythm and blues, was the fastest-growing segment of the record business.

Rhythm and Blues

Rhythm and blues, or R&B, began as an industry synonym for Chicago blues—the urban conflation of down-home Mississippi Delta blues, an African-derived folk idiom usually performed by a lone black man and his guitar, and the brassy swing of popular big band jazz. Pioneered by southern transplants such as Muddy Waters and fostered almost singlehandedly by the Chess record label, the Chicago tradition is kept alive today by such artists as "Son" Seals, Albert Collins, Albert King, Rhode Island's Roomful of Blues, and George Thorogood and the Delaware Destroyers.

The great blues shouter Howlin' Wolf traced the thin line dividing R&B from what came to be called rock and roll with the suggestion that "a twelve-bar and a four-bar intro, you're playing the blues. You step the stuff up and you're playing rock and roll." As performers of African heritage released an increasing number of disks in a variety of local dialects, R&B expanded to include virtually all of the black music of the forties and fifties, from the up-tempo boogie of jump bandsmen such as Louis Jordan to a cappella streetcorner doo-wop to the gospel-inflected vocal harmonizing of the Clovers.

Through the efforts of white fans such as Cleveland DJ-turned-promotor Alan Freed—who once tried unsuccessfully to copyright the phrase "rock and roll"—the music gained a foothold among white teenagers. In an odd parallel with the sit-ins and freedom rides of the civil rights struggle, more and more black clubs were finding it necessary to accommodate white teenagers. At first, they offered special "white nights." Later, they would divide the dance floor with a rope.

Industry Reaction

The R&B boom was a godsend for black entrepreneurs. The white-owned major labels dismissed "race music" as crude, lewd, and sure to go the way of the hula-hoop. So, like punk rock during the mid-seventies, the music was left to small, independent record labels, often black-owned and black-operated.

As the "indies," or independently owned record companies, ate steadily into the profits Columbia and RCA had been earning with crooners like Sammy Davis, Jr. and Frank Sinatra, the majors adopted a policy of containment. For every legitimate R&B hit, a cover version would appear—often a note-for-note replica, but with the rough edges sanded down—performed by a white artist. Pat Boone, safely outfitted in a letter sweater and white bucks, covered Fats Domino's "Ain't That a Shame." Meanwhile, Georgia Gibbs transformed Etta James' bawdy "Roll With Me, Henry" into "Dance With Me, Henry."

The trend was obvious. Even a small-time record producer like Sam Phillips, turning out classic R&B sides by the likes of B. B. King and Ike Turner from his own Sun Recording Studios in Memphis, Tennessee, realized that something big was about to happen. Phillips, one of the few white men who appreciated R&B as music, and one of the many willing to exploit it for his own financial benefit, was sitting in the Sun office one day when an idea came to him.

"If I could find a white man who had the Negro sound and the Negro feel," he mused to his secretary, "I could make a billion dollars." As if on cue, a young truck driver named Elvis Presley walked into Sun Studios in late 1953 to record some songs as a birthday present to his mother. As 1954 drew to a close, Phillips' first billion was beginning to roll in.

Opposite: The legendary Fats Domino, king of New Orleans R&B.

GREAT BALLS OF FIRE:

Sun Records and the Rockabilly Pioneers

He stood behind the mike for five minutes, I'll bet, before he made a move. Then he hit his guitar a lick and he broke two strings. So there he was, these two strings dangling, and he hadn't done anything yet, and these high school girls were screaming and fainting and running up onstage. And then he started to move his hips real slow like he had a thing for his guitar.

Bob Luman, country singer, describing an early concert appearance by Elvis Presley

The majors' strategy of recording white covers of R&B hits struck gold in June 1954. "Sh-Boom," originally by the Chords, became the first record ever to top both the R&B and pop charts in a new version by a Canadian group, the Crew Cuts.

A few months later, Bill Haley and the Comets released "Rock Around the Clock." The song wasn't a cover, but an original hit performed by a group composed entirely of white men. Often cited as the first example of bona fide rock and roll, it would go on to become the most successful rock and roll record of all time as part of the soundtrack for the teen-angst flick *Blackboard Jungle*.

But Sam Phillips was already at work creating a musical concoction of black and white that would take R&B far beyond the pop charts, into the hearts of America's youth and the ears of the entire world.

Elvis

© Bettmann Archives

In Elvis Presley, Phillips had found exactly what he was looking for: a white singer who could popularize the blues for the mainstream audience without sanitizing its bawdy, raucous spirit. The only child of a sharecropper and a seamstress, Elvis grew up on the poor side of Tupelo, Mississippi. By the time he was in high school, the Presleys had moved to Memphis and Elvis had taken on the trappings of a teen rebel: black clothing, sideburns, and a penchant for hanging out in nightclubs where R&B was performed. His charm, good looks, and pure animal magnetism impressed Phillips, but even more intriguing was his way, when he sang, of blending the country sounds of Roy Acuff and Ernest Tubb with the rhythms and sensuality of the Chicago blues.

A year after Presley first entered Sun Studios, his first single was on the charts: "That's All Right Mama," an R&B burner by Arthur "Big Boy" Crudup, backed with Bill Monroe's country hit, "Blue Moon of Kentucky." It was an explosive combination, calculated to make waves among both country aficionados and race music fans—and an explicit slap in the face to anyone who thought that the cultures of black and white should be kept apart. Onstage, Elvis, dressed in a green jacket, red pants, and a pink shirt with the collar turned up, leered at the audience. His initial tour of the South garnered outraged reviews and unprecedented fan hysteria at every stop.

Within a year, RCA had bought Presley's contract from Sun for $35,000—a pittance in retrospect, but at the time not an insubstantial sum. Simultaneously with his 1956 appearance on *The Ed Sullivan Show,* they released the throbbing "Heartbreak Hotel." Elvis skyrocketed to international fame, fortune, and idolatry. The classic hits that followed served as a virtual rock and roll blueprint for countless white singers, guitarists, drummers, bass players, and producers over the next decade: "Don't Be Cruel" and "Love Me Tender" in 1956, "All Shook Up," "Teddy Bear," and "Jailhouse Rock" in 1957, "Hard-Headed Woman" in 1958, "Big Hunk of Love" in 1959, and on and on.

By the time of his death in 1977, Elvis, depressed and drug-addicted, had become something of a bad joke. Amazingly, the joke has only become more elaborate with the passage of time, as evidenced by Elvis television serials, conventions of Elvis impersonators, and parodies such as the Residents' twisted history of rock and roll, *E Cubed*. Endless assertions in supermarket tabloids that the King's death was a hoax, and that he now enjoys a life of undisturbed anonymity, are belied by the recent issue of a U.S. postage stamp bearing his likeness—an honor for which ten years in the grave is a prerequisite. Such overwhelming success with the mainstream—in both its establishment and its lunatic-fringe manifestations—obscure Presley's pivotal role in rock and roll history.

Left and opposite: Elvis presented rock and roll to mass audiences, bringing what had been primarily African-American music to the ears of the entire world.

The Sun Records Stable

The new sound became known as "rockabilly," a contraction of rock and roll and hillbilly music (that is, country and bluegrass). Phillips found no shortage of white singers willing to sing the blues—mostly poor laborers of the socioeconomic stratum known as "white trash"—and over the next few years the Sun stable cut some of the greatest performances to bear the name of rock and roll. Jerry Lee Lewis injected blatant lust into Elvis' teen-idol sexuality in "Whole Lotta Shakin' Goin' on" (1957), "Great Balls of Fire" (1958), and "Breathless" (1958).

In "Get Rhythm" (1956), Johnny Cash acknowledged his debt to black street music years before rising to stardom in country music. Carl Perkins neatly summed up the value to poor white teenagers of a new pair of winkle-pickers in "Blue Suede Shoes" (1956), and forged the riffs that would propel Beatle George Harrison out of Liver-

pool and into the hearts of the entire world. In fact, George's audition for Paul and John, in 1958, consisted of playing "Raunchy" (1957) by Sun artist Bill Justis.

Buddy Holly

When RCA snapped up Elvis, the other major labels took notice. Decca countered by signing Buddy Holly, from Lubbock, Texas. As competition for Elvis, Holly cut an unlikely profile: tall and gangly, his trademark was a monstrous pair of black horn-rimmed glasses through which he looked myopically at the world. Holly was closer to a country singer than Presley; between 1954 and 1955 he had hosted a regular country show on KDAV radio.

After a few unsuccessful singles, Holly's "That'll Be the Day" (1957), based on a line spoken by John Wayne in *The Searchers,* was an immediate Number One in both the United States and the United Kingdom. Holly and his band, the Crickets, followed up with a steady stream of records marked by a wide-eyed buoyancy and earnest simplicity that few rockers have matched, including the classics "Peggy Sue" (1957), "Not Fade Away" (1957), "Rave on" (1958), and "Well Alright" (1958).

Over the next two years, Holly toured and recorded tirelessly, building a particularly fanatical following in Britain. Royalty disputes and other financial troubles, however, forced him onto the road once again during the harsh winter of 1958. Between dates in Clear Lake, Iowa, and Fargo, North Dakota, Holly and his tour mates and fellow rockers J. P. "Big Bopper" Richardson and Ritchie Valens chartered a plane in order to avoid the grueling bus ride. The weather was unrelenting, and the plane went down just after takeoff, killing all on board.

A minor star during his lifetime, Holly's stature has increased with each year since his death. As one of the few early rockers to write his own songs, he (along with Chuck Berry) paved the way for the Beatles and others who made direct self-expression one of rock's highest virtues. Selec-

tions from his remarkable catalog of songs, now owned by Paul McCartney, have been covered by a virtual rock and roll pantheon, including the Grateful Dead, the Rolling Stones, the Beatles, Blind Faith, and Linda Ronstadt. In the 1971 chart topper "American Pie," a nine-minute history of rock and roll, singer Don McLean referred obliquely to the date of Holly's plane crash as "the day the music died." McLean's estimation appears to be increasingly valid as the years pass.

Other Rockabilly Greats

Competition with Elvis spawned other rockabilly greats as well. Gene Vincent, popular in Britain but virtually unknown in North America, puzzled more literary-minded critics of popular culture with his 1956 hit "Be-Bop-a-Lula," inspired by a Little Lulu comic book. Hitting the charts in 1958 with "Summertime Blues," Eddie Cochran spoke eloquently for teenagers who were too young to vote, get a job, stay out late, and otherwise lead an independent existence. His career ended abruptly in 1960 with a car crash that also left Gene Vincent crippled for life. The Everly Brothers from Kentucky topped both the country and the pop charts simultaneously with "Bye Bye, Love" in 1957, singing in parallel harmonies that would have a profound influence on the Beatles, Simon & Garfunkel, and Crosby, Stills & Nash. More recently, the sound of rockabilly's pioneers was echoed by revivalists such as the Stray Cats and Ireland's Shakin' Pyramids.

While Elvis and his progeny were blending R&B with country, African-American performers were looking for ways to break through the barrier that kept black music off of the white charts. Experimenting with rhythms and arrangements, their aim was to develop a sound that the white-controlled music industry couldn't copy. During 1955, three black artists, each in his own separate way—Chuck Berry with "Maybelline," Little Richard with "Tutti Frutti," and Bo Diddley with a song named after himself—finally found it.

Buddy Holly.

FPG International

HAIL! HAIL! ROCK AND ROLL:

CLASSIC ROCK AND ROLL

Rock and roll is the most brutal, ugly, desperate, vicious form of expression it has been my misfortune to hear.

Frank Sinatra, testifying before Congressional payola hearings, 1958

Through his voice, clothing, and mannerisms, Elvis created an image of teen rebellion and erotic power that the white mainstream couldn't resist. In doing so, he broadened the market for rock and roll and inspired a generation of white musicians to play the blues, and for these achievements Elvis has been enthroned as the "King of Rock and Roll." But the crown belongs at least equally to Chuck Berry and Little Richard, and to a lesser extent to Bo Diddley.

As men of color, these three kings distilled their music more directly from the black experience. In the raw shuffle of R&B, they blended the big-band inflections of Louis Jordan's jumpin' jive, the rolling thunder of Southern Baptist revival meetings, the showmanship of medicine-show snake oil salesmen, and the intensity of African tribal ritual. They defined a palette of themes, rhythms, riffs, and attitudes from which rockers continue to draw to this day, forming the boundaries of classic rock and roll.

In the nineties, amazingly, all three artists are still on the scene: Little Richard with numerous film cameos and an early-nineties tour, Berry with a recent autobiography and the wonderful film portrait, *Hail! Hail! Rock and Roll,* and Diddley in Nike commercials with athlete Bo Jackson.

Chuck Berry

Of rock and roll's many brilliant pioneers, few shine as brightly as Chuck Berry. After a stint in a reformatory for attempted robbery, he worked as a cosmetologist and in an automobile factory before journeying to Chicago in 1955 in hopes of peddling his original songs. There, he had the great good fortune to join an impromptu jam session at a local club. As it happened, one of the participants was blues legend Muddy Waters, who was so impressed with Berry's guitar playing that he arranged an audition with his record label, Chess.

Berry recorded the up-tempo rocker "Maybelline" at his first session. Influential rock and roll DJ Alan Freed gave the record his best push (for which he received a songwriting credit and thus a share in the royalties) and, at the relatively advanced age of thirty, Berry found himself catapulted into the national limelight.

The hits that followed have gone on to become rehearsal and encore fodder for three generations of garage bands: "Roll Over Beethoven" (1956), "Brown-Eyed Handsome Man" (1956), "Rock and Roll Music" (1957), "Sweet Little Sixteen" (1958), "Johnny B. Goode" (1958), and "Nadine" (1964), to name only a few. On tour during the following

Chuck Berry.

Michael Ocns Archives

year, Berry played 101 consecutive concerts, thrilling audiences and perfecting his patented "duckwalk," a move in which he hopped across the stage on one leg while riffing furiously.

Aside from an armload of classic songs, Berry's contribution to rock and roll is twofold. As a songwriter, his work mapped the basic thematic terrain of early rock and roll, outlining a timeless teenage world of cars, transistor radios, dating, and hamburgers. His lyrics combine poetic incisiveness with a level of wit and humor reminiscent of Cole Porter, a trait especially missed in the nineties. And as a guitarist, Berry developed a library of distinctive licks—not country, not blues, but pure rock and roll—that have formed the stylistic bedrock of virtually every rock guitarist since.

Little Richard

If Berry bequeathed to rock and roll a basic musical and literary vocabulary, Richard Penniman— a.k.a. Little Richard—gave the music its sense of outrageous flamboyance. With his high pompadour hairdo, pencil-thin moustache, lipstick, and wide-open rolling eyeballs, Richard set the standard during the late fifties for sexual ambiguity and sheer rock and roll *chutzpah.* "People like Elvis Presley were the builders of rock and roll," he quipped in 1984, "but I was the architect."

Raised in a strict Seventh Day Adventist household in Macon, Georgia, young Richard toured as a child with scores of relatives as part of the Penniman Family, playing the piano and testifying the gospel. He made his first recordings in 1951 under the auspices of RCA after winning a talent contest, and by the mid-fifties was touring with Dr. Hudson's Medicine Show.

It was during these years that Little Richard began to perform his signature tune, a manic raveup called "Tutti Frutti." Richard shifted the standard R&B backbeat into high gear and smothered it with whoops, moans, and screams the likes of which had never been heard before (and rarely since). The song met with little response at the time of its release.

After a session during which Richard had laid down some blues tracks, he and his band ripped

through "Tutti Frutti" as a way of winding down. Record company executives rushed back into the studio to find out what the commotion was about, and insisted that it be captured on tape. The record hit the charts in early 1956, and Little Richard followed up with numerous screamers in the same fiery mold: "Long Tall Sally" (1956), "Ready Teddy" (1956), "Rip It Up" (1956), "Lucille" (1957), and "Good Golly Miss Molly" (1958, including the immortal lyric, "Good golly Miss Molly/You sure like to ball").

The hits piled up at breakneck speed until, in 1959, Richard saw the engines of his tour airplane burst into flames in midair. Supposedly, Little Richard watched as the fire was smothered by angels, and swore on the spot that he would dedicate his life to God if he reached the ground intact. He did, and in that year he left the stage—in front of 40,000 fans—to become a Seventh Day Adventist minister. By that time, however, his place in rock and roll history was assured.

Bo Diddley

Elias McDaniel, or Bo Diddley, stands not in the shadows of Berry and Richard, but off to one side. Growing up in Chicago, he was close to the wellspring of R&B, but where Berry and Richard brought an urbane sophistication to their interpretation of rock and roll, McDaniel's sound was rawer, more elemental, and both metaphorically and sociologically darker than theirs.

McDaniel landed his first nightclub gig in 1951. Four years later, he walked into the offices of Chess records and talked his way into an audition. This prompted the company's founder, Leonard Chess, to give him the name that would become famous—Bo Diddley—which means a teller of tall tales). Hunched intently over his trademark square-bodied guitar, he pounded out such classics as "Bo Diddley" (1955), "Mona" (1956), the timeless "Who Do You Love?" (1956), and "Crackin' Up" (1958).

Opposite: Rock and roll's first sexually ambiguous star, the dazzling Little Richard. Right: Bo Diddley pioneered the stomping rhythm now known as the "Bo Diddley beat."

All four songs employed a distinctive stomping rhythm based on three long accents followed by two short ones—a style that quickly became known as the "Bo Diddley beat." It's a groove that has been passed from musician to musician like a sacred talisman, appearing not only in covers by the Rolling Stones, the Yardbirds, the Animals, and others, but in the original work of contemporary artists as diverse as Elvis Costello ("Lover's Walk" from the album *Trust*) and George Michael ("Faith" from the album of the same name).

The other salient feature of Diddley's early recordings is the unearthly sound of his guitar. Although signal processing effects barely existed in the late fifties, he managed to wring an incredible variety of electronic sounds from his guitar using very limited means. Diddley was by no means a virtuosic player, but his penchant for exploring the sonic possibilities of the electric guitar marks him as the spiritual father of the instrument's supreme innovator, Jimi Hendrix.

But even as Berry, Richard, and Diddley were defining the scope of the new style, rock and roll was in grave danger. Reactionary forces had been gathering on the sidelines, waiting for the right moment to restore healthy values and old-fashioned good taste to American popular culture; by 1960, they had seized it.

Michael Ochs Archives

PUPPY LOVE:
THE REIGN OF THE TEEN IDOLS

P oised on the brink of the tumultuous sixties, rock and roll had become a force to be reckoned with. Radio stations and record labels struggled to rein the beast in and turn it to a purpose more worthwhile than making music (that is, making money). But it simply snarled more loudly, becoming increasingly intransigent with each new manifestation.

Beginning in 1959, however, teens throughout the world watched in amazement as a series of mishaps beset nearly every major rock and roll talent. First Buddy Holly, the Big Bopper, and Ritchie Valens perished in a plane crash. Then Eddie Cochran died. Gene Vincent, seriously injured in the car accident that took Cochran's life, left the stage for a hospital bed. Elvis had marched off to compulsory military duty, and Little Richard leaped onto the pulpit. Chuck Berry became embroiled in a trumped-up sex scandal that

Michael Ochs Archives

© BMI Photo Archives/Michael Ochs Archives

Fabian.

landed him in a federal pen for two years. Meanwhile, the lascivious Jerry Lee Lewis confirmed everyone's greatest fears by marrying his thirteen-year-old cousin, for which he was boycotted and banned from the airwaves.

The Philadelphia Sound

Into the breach jumped an all-American advertising-man-turned-TV-personality named Dick Clark. Since August 1957, Clark had hosted *American Bandstand,* the first effective translation of radio into the new medium of television. (Clark's show might be seen as the progenitor of MTV, which had to wait for the development of video and cable TV in order to happen). Not a great rock and roll fan, Clark nonetheless grasped the commercial potential of

the music and went about building an empire of TV shows, song copyrights, and record companies.

Bandstand, broadcast from Philadelphia, was a vehicle for a new breed of rock and roller, the safe-as-milk teen idol. This kind of star was perfectly suited to the major powers in the music industry. Teen idols had a predictable following, made music that lent itself to production-line manufacturing, and—above all—didn't offend the parents of fans, who tended to hold the purse strings. Through the likes of Fabian, Frankie Avalon, and Bobby Rydel, businessmen would tame the rock and roll beast.

The appeal of the teen idols was tailored to the hearts of affluent females of high-school age: handsome, well-groomed boys-next-door whose wholesomeness might be undercut by just a hint of mannered rebelliousness. Their hits—which defined the syrupy "Philadelphia Sound"—were produced by local factories that sprang up in the wake of *Bandstand's* success. The most successful was Cameo-Parkway, headed by Allen Klein, who would eventually manage both the Rolling Stones and the Beatles.

Companies like Cameo-Parkway gathered a house band, a studio, a label, and a promotion department under one umbrella. Clark picked the star, Cameo made the record, and *Bandstand* promoted the dance that went with it. (Cameo alone invented over thirty new dances—the Twist, the Pony, the Bristol Stomp, the Mashed Potato—each spearheaded by a single telling kids what the moves were.) It was an operation that couldn't fail, and during the years between the absence of Elvis and the advent of the British Invasion, it didn't.

Record labels around the country jumped on the bandwagon. New York's answer to the Philadelphia machines was ABC-Paramount, which groomed Paul Anka for success. In Los Angeles, Walt Disney tried to boost the curvaceous ex-Mouseketeer Annette Funicello into the charts. Television star Ricky Nelson ("I Wanna Be Loved," 1959) was one of the few teen idols to transcend the genre. Nelson's records boast an excellent band and songs written by rockabilly pioneer Johnny Burnette.

Payola and the Fall of Dick Clark

The reign of the teen idols came to an abrupt end in 1960 with Congressional inquiries into the record industry's methods of promotion. The scandals had begun in 1959 with fixed TV quiz shows and quickly spread throughout the entertainment world. Record companies, it turned out, were paying disc jockeys cash and even royalty percentages to play specific records, which inevitably would become hits. Clark figured heavily in the payola hearings, and eventually divested his holdings in thirty-three tainted companies. He continued to host *American Bandstand,* but without the necessary grease, the entire star-making machinery no longer ran so smoothly.

The coast was now clear for the arrival of the sixties.

Opposite, top: Dick Clark (far right) on the set of *American Bandstand.*

BEFORE THE BIG TIME

Here is a look at what some of rock and roll's stars did for a living before they became famous for their music.

Frank Beard (ZZ Top)	Sporting-goods salesman	Dr. John	Ivory Soap baby
Pat Benatar	Bank teller	Grace Jones	Model
Chuck Berry	Hairdresser, beautician	Tom Jones	Glove cutter
David Bowie	Model, art teacher	Jon Bon Jovi	7-Eleven clerk
James Brown	Cotton picker	Cyndi Lauper	Racehorse walker
Eric Burdon	Mailman	Annie Lennox	Waitress
Belinda Carlisle	Gas-station attendant	Madonna	Burger King employee
George Clinton	Barber	Bette Midler	Pineapple-cannery worker, go-go dancer
Alannah Currie (Thompson Twins)	Tobacco picker		
		Keith Moon	Plaster salesman
Roger Daltrey	Sheetmetal worker	Stevie Nicks	Bob's Big Boy hostess
Bernard Edwards (Chic)	Postal clerk	Elvis Presley	Usher, truck driver
Jon Elliot (Def Leppard)	Van driver	Lou Reed	Assistant in accounting firm
Perry Farrell	Vitamin-factory worker	Keith Richards	Postal clerk
David Gilmour	Model	Sade	Bicycle messenger
Peter Gabriel	Travel-agency assistant	Rod Stewart	Grave digger
Boy George	Clothing-store clerk	Sting	School teacher
Hammer	Bat boy for the Oakland A's	Sly Stone	Radio D.J.
Debbie Harry	Beautician	Tina Turner	Cotton picker
Screamin' Jay Hawkins	Prizefighter	Lars Ulrich (Metallica)	Tennis player
Chris Isaak	Tour guide in Japan	Tom Waits	Vacuum-cleaner salesman
Mick Jagger	Ice-cream salesman	David Wakeling (English Beat)	Bingo caller
		Peter Wolf	Radio D.J.

FUN, FUN, FUN:
SURFER BOYS AND GIRL GROUPS

I n Los Angeles, the escapist tone of the Philadelphia star factories ripened in the warm California sun. Southern California had always been something of a mythical paradise to the rest of America, particularly to the young, who consumed voraciously the area's primary exports: movies and television shows. At the close of the fifties, L.A.'s inbred affluence and hedonism fostered a teen culture that revolved around surfing. Beach-party movies were the inevitable result; equally inevitable was that the beaches of Los Angeles would become the stage for one of the era's great musical fads, surf rock.

The early surf hits were instrumentals, compositions that converted staple rock and roll riffs into shuddering expressions of the excitement of riding the perfect wave. Among the standouts were "Tequila" (the Champs, 1958), "Walk—Don't Run" (the Ventures, 1960), "Wipe Out" (the Surfaris, 1963), and "Pipeline" (the Chantays, 1963). But it took the genius of the Beach Boys to transform surf culture into a wave the entire nation could catch.

The Beach Boys

There were no more articulate spokesmen for the West coast youth subculture than the Beach Boys. Celebrating the pleasures of being young, wealthy, and Californian in glorious barbershop vocal harmonies, they conjured up a teen utopia in which there were "two girls for every boy" and the primary activities were surfing, drag racing, and necking. "Surfin' Safari" was their first national hit in 1962, followed by "Surfin' U.S.A" (1963, a thinly disguised ripoff of Chuck Berry's "Sweet Little Sixteen") and "Fun, Fun, Fun" (1964).

For the touching ballad "Surfer Girl" (1963), leader Brian Wilson took over production duties. From that moment, the Beach Boys moved beyond teen myth making to transcend the genre they had helped to define. Over the next several years, they created some of the most expressive songs in all of rock and roll, including "In My Room" (1963), "Don't Worry Baby" (1964), "California Girls" (1965), "Wouldn't It Be Nice" (1966), and their crowning achievement, "Good Vibrations" (1966).

The Girl Groups

The Beach Boys sang in male voices to other boys, while the teen idols, almost invariably young men, had aimed their messages straight at the hearts of the fairer sex. The girl groups that rose to prominence during the early sixties, including the Chantels, the Crystals, the Shirelles, and the Marvelettes, offered female listeners stars that they could relate to directly. Unlike the Beach Boys, who were a harbinger of things to come, and the teen idols, who were largely a throwback to the crooners of a bygone era, the girl groups evolved directly from the black gospel tradition of (male) vocal quartets—the music that, when fused with R&B, would spontaneously combust into soul during the early sixties.

Girl group music was, in the most intimate sense, by teenage girls and for teenage girls. ("Get the picture?" the narrator asks in "Leader of the Pack" by the Shangri-Las. "Yes, we see," her girlfriends reply in unison.) The songs invariably were about the thing that matters most in life: teenage boys. It was a music of passionate yearning and youthful dreams that would leave behind some of the most memorable hits of the early sixties, including "Baby It's You" and "Dedicated to the One I Love" by the Shirelles (1961), "Da Do Ron Ron" and "Then He Kissed Me" by the Crystals (1963), the Angels' "My Boyfriend's Back" (1963), "Be My Baby" by the Ronettes (1963), "Chapel of Love" by the Dixie Cups (1964), and "He's So Fine" by the Chiffons (1963, which George Harrison was accused of copying in a plagiarism suit involving his "My Sweet Lord" in 1971).

Phil Spector and the Wall of Sound

The best of the girl group records were produced by eccentric *wunderkind* Phil Spector. Arriving on the music scene when he was just seventeen, Spector introduced the notion that a record's producer could be more important, artistically speaking, than its singer, songwriter, or band. Spector's specialty was the "wall of sound," a glorious din capable of escalating the starry eyes of a first date into an ecstatic drama of epic proportions. He called his productions "little symphonies for the kids." At the dawn of the sixties, Spector and the girl groups ushered in a new era, an age in which—for better or worse— even the most popular of popular music could be thought of as high art.

Opposite: The Beach Boys. Above: Phil Spector and two of the Ronettes.

Michael Ochs Archives

Combining the gospel stylings of Sam Cooke with the intensity of Little Richard, Otis Redding was one of the primary architects of soul.

LAND OF A THOUSAND DANCES:

MEMPHIS AND THE SOUL EXPLOSION

For all its popularity, the blues during the forties and fifties was still regarded as the "Devil's music" by many African-Americans. Religious music and secular music didn't mix in earnest until, with the dawn of the civil rights movement, the more progressive elements of the black community emerged.

As the fifties came to a close, Ray Charles, Sam Cooke, and James Brown—all born in the early thirties or before—were recording back-slidden gospel songs for the R&B market. But they didn't sell as well as songs without a gospel influence. Singers a decade or so younger, though, cross-pollinated their gospel with rock and roll rather than R&B. They adopted a more solid beat, one that jelled R&B's swinging shuffle into a hard-driving urban stomp, and their audiences screamed for more. When Solomon Burke (born c. 1940) released his rocking "Just Out of Reach" in 1961, disc jockeys labelled the sound "rock 'n' soul." That record signalled the arrival of soul as a full-scale movement.

Along with Solomon Burke, Otis Redding and Wilson Pickett were the primary architects of the new sound.

Otis Redding

Born in Dawson, Georgia in 1941, the young Otis Redding performed at college fraternity parties throughout the South as a member of Johnny Jenkins & the Pinetoppers. When Jenkins eventually landed a solo contract, he asked Redding to drive him to the first recording session. During the half hour that was left after he had finished recording, Jenkins invited Redding to record a few tunes. Redding was signed on the spot.

Redding's two biggest influences were screamer Little Richard and gospel star Sam Cooke, and his first album contains many imitations of the former and covers of the latter. His gentle, quivering voice displayed its greatest power, however, in ballads. Masterful examples include "I've Been Loving You Too Long" (1965) and "That's How Strong My Love Is" (1965, covered by the Rolling Stones in 1965 and by Bryan Ferry in 1980). "Respect" (1965), later a breakthrough smash for Aretha Franklin, found Redding experimenting with a harder rocking style.

By 1967, Redding's following with black Americans was fanatical, and he had gained a reputation throughout Europe as a dramatic stage performer. *Dictionary of Soul,* his 1966 offering, was hailed as an instant classic, and his appearance at the Monterey Pop Festival was immortalized in vinyl as *Monterey International Pop Festival: Otis Redding/The Jimi Hendrix Experience* (one side of Redding, the other of Hendrix). Tragically, his career ended abruptly in a plane crash over the Midwest on December 10, 1967. The song for which he is best known today, "(Sittin' on) The Dock of the Bay," was released posthumously.

Wilson Pickett

It was Redding's tough sound on Stax Records, which came to be known as Memphis soul (recorded at Stax annexes in Memphis and Muscle Shoals, Alabama), that prompted Atlantic executives to bring Wilson Pickett to record with the Stax team in 1965. Pickett and Stax couldn't have been a better match. With his raspy voice and fireball delivery, Pickett sang over the rock-solid backing of Stax's house band, Booker T. & the MGs. Their first collaboration, "In the Midnight Hour" (1965) became the best-selling soul record of all time. The hits that followed sound as inspired today as they did then: "Mustang Sally" (1966), "Ninety-Nine and a Half" (1966), "Land of a Thousand Dances" (1966), and many others.

The Soul Explosion

As Pickett and Redding were cutting their first hits, it was becoming clear that the civil rights movement couldn't change America overnight. Soon the black community's greatest leaders, Martin Luther King and Malcolm X, would be slain before the eyes of the world, and violence would erupt in urban ghettos across America. Amidst the turmoil, the word "soul" became a trademark of black identity: suddenly there were soul brothers and soul sisters, soul food, and Eldridge Cleaver's *Soul on Ice.* Soul music became a way to reclaim black culture from the likes of Elvis and the Beatles, who had usurped it when it was called R&B.

The resulting creative ferment gave black artists a chance to cross over into the white mainstream in a way that had been inconceivable only a few years before. The close of the sixties saw a veritable "soul explosion," playing an earthy counterpoint to the white community's psychedelia. Fed by the earlier successes of the girl groups, the explosion was ignited when the mounting momentum of Memphis soul and Motown, as well as independents such as Al Green, met the newfangled funk of James Brown and Sly Stone. One performer, however, lit the match: Aretha Franklin, the "First Lady of Soul."

Aretha Franklin

Perhaps the greatest gospel performer of the postwar era was Mahalia Jackson, whose music plays a prominent role in the soundtrack of Spike Lee's 1991 film *Jungle Fever.* Jackson's soulful spirit inspired Aretha Franklin at a very early age. As the daughter of an evangelical minister, Franklin allied herself with gospel music until it became clear that a gospel background could lead to success in popular music.

John Hammond, her mentor at Columbia Records (soon to sign Bob Dylan), compared Franklin to the woman considered the greatest jazz vocalist of all time, calling hers "the best voice I've heard since Billie Holiday." For her first recordings in 1960, however, Hammond shoehorned her into a Barbra Streisand mold, assigning her show tunes adorned with lush orchestrations. The results didn't sit well with either the singer or her audience, and Franklin moved over to Atlantic's legendary soul stable.

Atlantic's hard-rocking style suited Franklin's penchant for ecstatic shouts and gospel preaching, and the public listened up. Her first single, "I Never Loved a Man," rose to Number One in late 1966, followed by the smash hits "Respect," "Baby, I Love You," and "Chain of Fools" in 1967. The following year's output was equally brilliant, and established Aretha as one of the world's greatest singers in any style. Periodic hits such as "Until You Come Back to Me" (1974), "Freeway of Love" (1985), and "Through the Storm" (1989, with Elton John) continue to demonstrate her vocal mastery.

The soul explosion, mirrored by Franklin's popularity, put black artists on equal footing with whites in the hearts of the world's teenagers. Soon thereafter, however, the soul scene began to fragment. Regional scenes sprang up, particularly in Chicago and Philadelphia. The music's more popular elements mingled with mainstream pop, while its dance-floor offshoot became disco.

In the nineties, soul infuses nearly every corner of mainstream pop and rock, from the Top Ten hits of Whitney Houston, Terence Trent D'Arby, and Luther Vandross to the dance-floor pop of Madonna, Jody Watley, and Bobby Brown to the sounds of Afro-America's latest innovation, rap.

"The First Lady of Soul," Aretha Franklin.

HOW SWEET IT IS:
THE GOLDEN ERA OF MOTOWN

While soul power was cutting a deep groove in Stax's studios and Atlantic's executive suite, a parallel development was taking place in Detroit, Michigan. Blending the same gospel and R&B influences, a young song-writer named Berry Gordy tempered his soulful stylings with a remarkably acute pop sensibility. After composing a few minor hits for R&B legend Jackie Wilson, Gordy got into production, selling his masters in New York to clients who turned out to be less than scrupulous when it came to details like royalty payments.

Gordy was after big-time commercial success, but his primary goal was independence from the racially lopsided structure of the music business at the time. Taking out a loan in 1959, he founded the company that would by 1966 score an aston-ishing 75 percent of the hits on the U.S. charts: Motown Records (first called Tammi, then Tamla, and still later incorporating Gordy, Soul, V.I.P., and Rare Earth divisions).

Like the production houses that created the teen idols of Philadelphia, Motown was con-ceived as a hit factory. Gordy controlled his artists' careers from soup to nuts, integrating management, songwriting, instrumental accom-paniment, recording, packaging, and distribution under one roof. Motown stars were even kept on an allowance in order to curb their appetites for gambling, intoxicants, and extravagant posses-sions, and Gordy incorporated a finishing school to groom his stars for acceptance among middle-class white audiences.

The most amazing aspect of Gordy's operation is that it produced great music. Motown's com-posers, under the direction of the crack team Holland-Dozier-Holland, were unfailingly inventive even as they were unabashedly formulaic. The anonymous house band, often anchored by Maurice White on drums (later the founder of funk sophisticates Earth, Wind & Fire), rivalled the best of the day. Motown's reserve of talented singers was seemingly inexhaustible, and Gordy's pro-ducers consistently coaxed inspired performances out of them.

Motown Classics

Simply to list all of the Motown classics would fill pages. Their immense appeal is amply demon-strated, though, by the numerous cover versions

Michael Ochs Archives

Berry Gordy, the founder of Motown Records.

that continue to swamp the charts. For example, Motown's first million-seller, "You Really Got a Hold on Me" (1962), appeared on the Beatles' second album. Martha & the Vandellas' "Heat Wave" (1963) became a hit for Linda Ronstadt in 1975, as did Smokey Robinson's "The Tracks of My Tears" (1965). "Just My Imagination" (1971) by the Temptations was covered by the Rolling Stones about a decade later.

In 1967, comedian Bill Cosby recorded Stevie Wonder's 1966 hit "Uptight (Everything's Alright)." James Taylor took Marvin Gaye's "How Sweet It Is (To Be Loved By You)" (1964) back to the top of the charts in 1975. And the Jackson Five's ever-green "Never Can Say Goodbye" (1971) seems to be revamped for every new fashion in dance music, most recently by the Communards in 1988.

In the first flush of the late-seventies new wave, the English Beat gave Robinson's "Tears of a Clown" (1965) a lilting Jamaican ska groove. Meanwhile, the British technopop duo Soft Cell scored with the Supremes' "Where Did Our Love Go"—paired with their own "Tainted Love," during the early eighties, followed by Phil Collins' remake of the Supremes' "You Can't Hurry Love." The Jackson Five's timeless debut, "I Want You Back" (1969), was revived by Graham Parker & the Rumour in 1980.

A few years later, the California Raisins made a novelty hit out of Marvin Gaye's smoldering "I Heard it Through the Grapevine" (1968). Motown hits are periodically revived through television spe-cials such as *Motown's 25th Anniversary* and mov-ies like *The Big Chill.* All of which fails to note the singular achievements of Motown luminaries the Four Tops, Junior Walker & the All Stars, the Marvelettes, and Gladys Knight & the Pips.

The superstar solo careers of Diana Ross and Michael Jackson demonstrate that Motown artists were capable of transcending their genre. But from a distance of nearly twenty years, the true Titans of Motown appear to have been Stevie Wonder and Marvin Gaye.

Clockwise from the top: Motown's suave Temptations, their more successful female counterparts the Supremes, and the silken-voiced Smokey Robinson & the Miracles. The Motown stable adapted raw soul for the mass market, dominating the record charts during the mid-1960s.

This page: Stevie Wonder. Opposite: Marvin Gaye.

Stevie Wonder

Blind from birth, Steveland Morris began life in 1950 in Saginaw, Michigan. It was obvious during his earliest years that he was extraordinarily gifted in music, and had impressed Berry Gordy sufficiently to land a contract. His first album, *Little Stevie Wonder, 12 Year Old Genius*—a live recording—hit the charts in 1963 and yielded the hit single, "Fingertips, Part 2." The Rolling Stones opened for the young prodigy during his 1964 tour. (He returned the favor, opening for them in 1972).

Wonder's musical alchemy turned into gold an amazing variety of material throughout the sixties, including Las Vegas pop ("For Once in My Life," 1968), syrupy ballads ("My Cherie Amour," 1969), Bob Dylan's "Blowin' in the Wind" (1966), and the protofunk of his first self-penned hit in 1966, "Uptight (Everything's Alright)." He didn't really come into his own until 1970, when he broke Motown precedent by producing his own album, the soul landmark *Signed, Sealed, and Delivered.*

SSD presaged the dramatic turning point in Wonder's career. After reaching legal status as an adult in 1971, he renegotiated his contract and wrested complete creative control from the Motown production team. With his newfound freedom, Wonder produced a series of groundbreaking albums on which he wrote, produced, and played virtually all of the instruments: *Music of My Mind* and *Talking Book* (1972), *Innervisions* (1973), *Fulfillingness' First Finale* (1974), and *Songs in the Key of Life* (1976). These albums had a formative impact on the stylistic evolution of funk, at the same time establishing Stevie Wonder as one of the major figures in pop music, black or white.

In the summer of 1973, a log fell from a truck driving in front of Wonder's car and careened through his windshield, hitting him in the head. The accident didn't take his life, but it left him without a sense of smell. Apparently, his musicianship was unaffected. Still, Wonder's post-1976 records have been far less significant, despite periodic chart toppers that include "Ebony and Ivory" (1982, with Paul McCartney), "I Just Called to Say I Love You" (1984), and "Part-Time Lover" (1985). Via contributions such as his 1991 theme to Spike Lee's film *Jungle Fever,* he remains active as an elder statesman of black pop.

Marvin Gaye

The son of a minister, Marvin Gaye had recorded with various doo-wop vocal groups on the Okeh and Chess labels when he married Berry Gordy's sister, Anna. At first, Motown hired him as a session drummer. But by 1963 he had topped the charts as a soloist with "Can I Get a Witness."

Graced with chiseled features and a suave demeanor, Gaye was perfectly suited for the role of Motown's resident beefcake idol. Throughout the years, he cut a series of steamy duets with stablemates Mary Wells, Tammi Terrell, Kim Weston, and Diana Ross, sentimental odes to an elusive ideal of romantic love. With Terrell's death during brain surgery in 1970, though, Gaye sank into a depression that threatened to end his career.

Inspired by Stevie Wonder's example, Gaye declared his independence from the Motown machinery in 1971 with a self-penned and self-produced effort, *What's Going on.* The album, an integrated cycle of topical laments, had no precedent. In subdued ruminations such as "Inner City Blues" and "Mercy Mercy Me (the Ecology)," Gaye translated his suffering into heartfelt concern for all humanity. (The album's title song became a hit once again for Robert Palmer in 1991.) With the follow-up, *Let's Get It on* (1973), Gaye raised rock and roll's usual celebration of eroticism to an apex of sensitivity and honesty. Although less influential than Wonder's records, these two are among the most satisfying albums in rock.

Beset by financial and personal troubles, Gaye's career declined throughout the seventies. He returned to the charts in 1981 with "Sexual Healing," but sadly, the comeback was short-lived. In a bizarre tragedy, he was shot to death by his father in 1984. Gaye's life is eulogized in "Missing You" (1984) by Diana Ross and "Nightshift" (1985) by Motown latecomers the Commodores.

Although Motown artists continue to make hits in the nineties, the label's golden period was over by the mid-seventies. Echoes of vintage Motown, however, can be heard in the music of mid-eighties blue-eyed soul chart toppers such as Hall & Oates and Phil Collins, and more recently in the hits of the Fine Young Cannibals.

JACKIE WILSON SAYS:
BLUE-EYED SOUL AND R&B

As early as 1962, Bill Medley and Bobby Hatfield, both white Californians, were copying the soul stylings of black artists. Initially, they had their greatest success with black audiences, who paid them a supreme compliment by describing their sound as "righteous." As the Righteous Brothers, they coined the term "blue-eyed soul," using the phrase as the title of their second album in 1964. In 1965, they emerged from an unprecedented three weeks in the studio with producer Phil Spector. The fruit of their efforts was "You've Lost That Lovin' Feeling," one of the greatest soul records of all time.

The Righteous Brothers weren't a record-company confabulation designed to soak up dollars that otherwise would flow into the black community. Like the blues revivalists of early-sixties London, the best of the white soulmen paid sincere tribute to proto-soul giants such as Jackie Wilson and Ray Charles, and sought to further the style by their own talents.

Through their inevitable synthesis of black and white, blue-eyed soul artists served as a Trojan horse, smuggling the sounds of African-American music into the white mainstream. By the late eighties, a huge portion of the best-selling records would bear a marked soul influence.

The Rascals and Steve Winwood

The Young Rascals continued the righteous tradition with "Good Lovin'" (1966) and "Groovin'" (1967). In the United Kingdom, the Spencer Davis Group churned out "Gimme Some Lovin'" (1967), powered by sixteen-year-old Steve Winwood. Winwood went on to form major sixties groups Traffic and Blind Faith, and topped the charts once again during the late eighties with the hits "Higher Love" (1987) and "Roll With It" (1988).

Joe Cocker

Hailed during the late sixties as one of the great voices of white soul, Joe Cocker crooned the Beatles' "With a Little Help From My Friends" (1968) in his best Ray Charles growl. Unfortunately, he never lived up to the promise of his early releases. Incidentally, both Cocker and Bill Medley found their careers revived during the early eighties by film score duets with Jennifer Warnes. Cocker's was "Up Where We Belong" from *An Officer and a Gentleman* (1983). Medley belted out "(I've Had) The Time of My Life" in *Dirty Dancing* (1987).

Van Morrison

The greatest white soul singer to emerge from the sixties was a chubby Irishman named George Ivan Morrison, better known as Van Morrison. With his Ulster-based group, Them, Morrison brought the voice of a Chicago blues shouter to the underground classics "Baby Please Don't Go" and "Gloria" (both 1964). The band never took off, though, and Morrison embarked on a solo career.

After an initial pop-rock hit, "Brown-Eyed Girl" (1967), Morrison turned out a series of brilliant albums that delivered soulful R&B with an introspective bent, notably *Astral Weeks* (1968), *Moondance* (1970), *Tupelo Honey* (1971), and

Veedon Fleece (1974). Since then, Morrison has maintained a low-profile career, exploring a characteristically Irish mysticism that draws on the inherent spirituality of soul music.

Creedence Clearwater Revival

Morrison's American counterpart was Creedence Clearwater Revival from Northern California. Creedence's style owed much to rockabilly and Louisiana Cajun sounds, but the group's early hits boasted African-American roots: raging covers of Dale Hawkins' "Suzy Q," "I Put a Spell on You" by Screamin' Jay Hawkins, and Little Richard's "Good Golly Miss Molly" (all 1968), as well as the classic original "Proud Mary" (1969). The latter was acknowledged in cover versions by none other than Solomon Burke and Ike & Tina Turner. Creedence's later hits included "Bad Moon Rising" (1969), "Down on the Corner" (1969), "Up Around the Bend" (1970), "Have You Ever Seen the Rain" (1971), and "Sweet Hitchhiker" (1971).

Hall & Oates and Robert Palmer

The seeds of white soul in the eighties were sown in Philadelphia during the heyday of Philly soul. Daryl Hall, the son of two classical musicians, divided his time evenly between singing with the Philadelphia Orchestra and sessions for Gamble & Huff's Philadelphia International label. Meanwhile, John Oates recorded with Kenny Gamble & the Romeos, one of a number of local groups made up of session players.

Hall & Oates gigged together as a folk duo during the late sixties, but they hit the big time with the soulful "She's Gone" in 1973. Soon, the duo was turning out sweet soul music nonstop with

"Sara Smile" (1975), "Rich Girl" (1977), "One on One" (1983), the Motown cop "Maneater" (1983), "Method of Modern Love" (1984), and "Everything Your Heart Desires" (1988). The duo's unerring instinct for melody and natural grasp of Top-Forty fashion produced some of the most satisfying hits of the decade.

Britain's answer to Hall & Oates may well be Robert Palmer. Ever careful to maintain his playboy image, Palmer started by recording songs in a broad range of styles, slowly working his way into a sophisticated soul groove ("You Are in My System"). By 1986, he had perfected a unique hard-rocking formula that yielded "Addicted to Love" and "I Didn't Mean to Turn You on." These hits, along with his association with ex-members of Duran Duran as part of Power Station ("Get It on," 1985), secured Palmer's status as one of the top stars of the eighties.

David Bowie

By the time he became the world's premier white soul star, David Bowie had already plied his talents as mime, commercial artist, teen idol (under his given name, David Jones—he switched to Bowie when the Monkees turned out to have their own David Jones), space alien weirdo, ace producer, and glitter-rock pioneer. When he recorded *Young Americans* in Philadelphia in 1975, it seemed that he had finally found an artistic identity that he felt comfortable with.

The hits from that album, the sardonic title cut and the bitter "Fame" (a James Brown ripoff credited to Bowie and John Lennon) were funky and down-to-earth, a welcome relief from the anguished themes of Bowie's previous records. *Station to Station* offered more of the same in 1976, featuring "Golden Years." During the remainder of the decade, though, Bowie embarked on the intensive art-rock phase of his career.

The Thin White Duke returned in 1983 with the triumphant *Let's Dance,* produced by Chic's Nile Rodgers. The record updated Bowie's earlier funk excursions for the new decade, pounding with a joyful beat and achieving massive sales.

Although subsequent releases have found Bowie back in his rock and roll shoes, his soul period was tremendously influential in bringing to a close the "disco sucks" era, which virtually locked funky grooves out of the American Top Forty.

Phil Collins

When Phil Collins made his first solo album in 1981, he had already spent a decade as peerless drummer, and later dynamic frontman, for the progressive rock group Genesis. Surprisingly, *Face Value* presented Collins as a natural pop star with an affection for Stax and Motown.

His debt to art rock showed on the album's standout, "In the Air Tonight." But on "I Missed Again," Earth, Wind & Fire's muscular brass section punched and stabbed over an infectious groove. On the strength of hits such as "You Can't Hurry Love" (1982), "Easy Lover" (1984), and "Sussudio" (1985), Collins' classy white soul has become a staple of playlists the world over.

George Michael

While Collins was well into middle age when he first hit the charts, George Michael was a huge star in the United Kingdom while he was still in high school. As the dominant half of the slick teenybopper duo Wham!, Michael cracked the States wide open in 1984 with a surprisingly mature set of soul-flavored pop hits, including "Careless Whisper," "Everything She Wants," and "Wake Me Up Before You Go Go."

In 1987, he emerged with a more grown-up image, as well as a controversial single. Demurely titled "I Want Your Sex," the song was banned on many North American radio stations, but managed, of course, to become a huge hit anyway. Given the consistency of Michael's smash albums *Faith* and *Listen Without Prejudice,* it seems likely that he'll be playing a role in the cutting-edge pop of the nineties.

Fine Young Cannibals and Was (Not Was)

And yet, the nineties are shaping up as an era that favors a less polished approach than that of George Michael, Phil Collins, Robert Palmer, or Hall & Oates. The Fine Young Cannibals, an outgrowth of ska revivalists the English Beat, temper their hits with a dash of punk attitude, leaving a prickly border of rough edges around otherwise immaculate soul-rock gems. "She Drives Me Crazy" (1989) worked Roland Gift's rasping, Jaggeresque voice and racially ambiguous sex appeal to brilliant effect, establishing the Cannibals as a major group, and portending great things from them in coming years.

Likewise, Was (Not Was) sends soulful ballads and crazed rock and roll careening into a head-on collision with chart-topping results. Known for wacky soul novelties featuring cameos by the likes of Mel Torme, leaders David "Was" Weiss and Don "Was" Fagenson enlisted the support of black vocal dynamos Sweet Pea Atkinson and Sir Harry Bowens for the hit "Walk the Dinosaur" (1989). On the strength of the accompanying album, *What Up, Dog?,* Fagenson was invited to produce records for Bonnie Raitt (the Grammy-laden *Nick of Time*) and Iggy Pop (*Brick by Brick*). Lighthearted but by no means lightweight, Was (Not Was) evinces a refreshing good-time sensibility without sacrificing the music's razor-sharp edge.

Originally a white homage to the black soul pioneers, over the years blue-eyed soul has emerged as a distinct subgenre, along the way becoming a major tributary to mainstream rock. While Hall & Oates, Robert Palmer, and the like have played an important role both in popularizing and infusing soul with a more up-to-date approach, groups like Was (Not Was) and the Fine Young Cannibals are dissolving the boundaries that separate black from white in a more direct manner. Under their influence, the nineties may turn out to be the decade in which rock and roll finally becomes the color-blind art form that, beneath the skin, it always has been.

SATISFACTION:
BRITISH INVASION/
AMERICAN DEFENSE

So this is America? They all seem out of their minds.

Ringo Starr, 1964, reacting to the mob that greeted the Beatles upon their arrival at JFK airport

Dick Clark, Phil Spector, the Beach Boys, and early Motown filled an obvious gap in pop music for white American teenagers. They were a weak substitute, though, for the kind of rebellious independence that Elvis had offered their older brothers and sisters. In England, however, Elvis had never really arrived. Government-sponsored radio and television presented only government-approved entertainment, and British pop during the early sixties was as calculatingly inoffensive as Dick Clark's Philadelphia Sound.

In the English port town of Liverpool, American rock and roll, R&B, and soul records passed into the hands of teenagers via sailors who stopped off in the States. The American sound was raw, tough, intolerable to the British mainstream—perfect for kids who, given Britain's staggeringly depressed economy, had little to do but fight in the streets and play rock and roll. Fusing the intensity of black American music with the desperation of British youth, the Liverpool sound touched a raw nerve. By 1962 the local music scene was a writhing mass of "beat groups" and "beat clubs."

It was a startling development—British youth creating a culture authentically their own, rather than having it handed to them on a vinyl platter—that spread to London, Manchester, and other major cities in England, spawning similar bands throughout the U.K. As they gained popularity in their own country, bands were exported to America in droves: the Rolling Stones, the Who, the Kinks, the Animals, the Hollies, the Yardbirds, the Dave Clark Five, the Moody Blues, the Zombies (the predecessor of Argent), and Them (from Ireland, featuring the young Van Morrison). Spearheading the British Invasion, of course, were the incomparable Beatles.

The Beatles

Although they looked to the world like a rags-to-riches story, the Beatles are a textbook example of the fact that raw talent and hard work are the two essential ingredients of musical success—and that being in the right place at the right time runs a close third. After slogging through the Liverpool club scene for a few years, John Lennon, Paul McCartney, George Harrison, and drummer Pete Best achieved some success in Hamburg, where the denizens of the notorious Reeperbahn red-light district displayed an insatiable appetite for British bands.

Back in Liverpool, the band landed a contract with the backwater Parlophone label, signed on drummer Ringo Starr, and proceeded to hammer Britain with concerts, radio appearances, and publicity stunts. Meanwhile, a series of great singles, including the transcendent "Please Please Me" (1963), rose to the top of the U.K. charts. For

FPG International

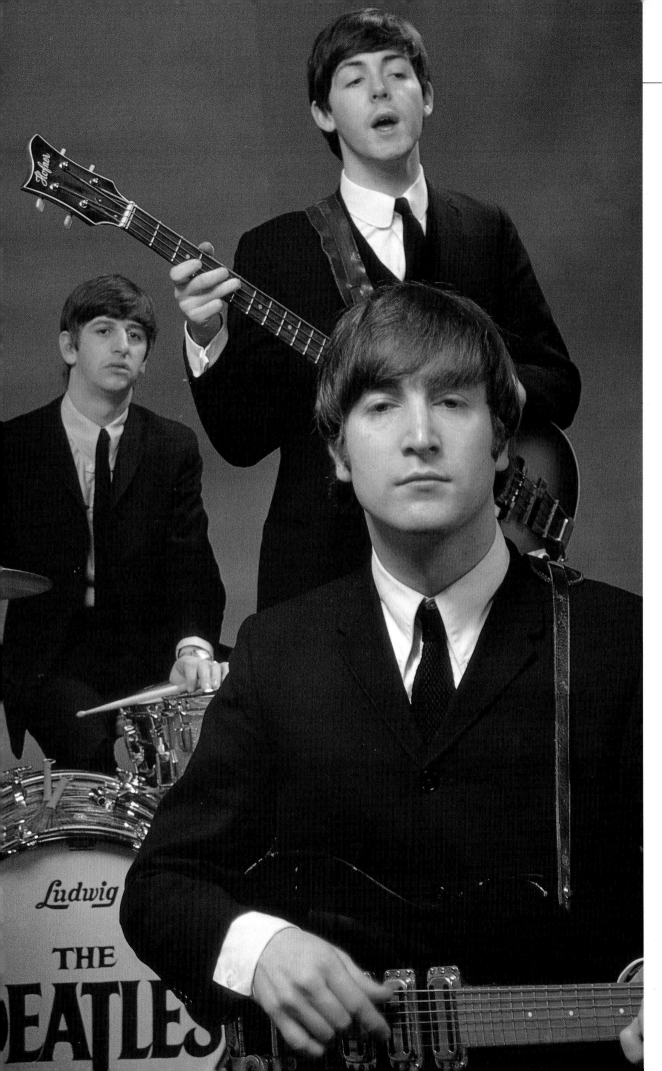

their arrival in America in early 1964, the Beatles were preceded by one of the most aggressive and well-coordinated publicity campaigns ever devised by a record company. They charmed Americans young and old alike on television's *The Ed Sullivan Show,* and the simultaneous release of "I Want to Hold Your Hand" (1964) catapulted the Fab Four to international fame.

The Beatles' music was a summation of virtually every major stylistic trait yet manifested in rock and roll: the big beat of Chicago blues, the manic energy of Little Richard, the supreme songwriting craftsmanship of Chuck Berry, the vocal harmonies of the Everly Brothers, the sex appeal of the teen idols, the lyricism of the Beach Boys, and the romantic intensity of the girl groups. To all of that, they added a level of wit, musical

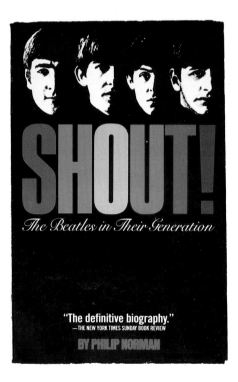

The Beatles' impact in America was substantial enough to rate the covers of nearly every mainstream news periodical, including *Life* and *Newsweek.*

Right: The Beatles.

openness, and uncompromising adventurousness that was entirely new. The coming years found them setting trends in everything from hairstyles to political opinion to religious philosophy, while each new record was a quantum leap beyond the last.

The Fab Four managed to ride the crest of every major wave of popular culture. With *Rubber Soul* (1965), pop music became fodder for serious criticism. *Revolver* (1966) and *Sgt. Pepper's Lonely Hearts Club Band* (1967) used the resources of the recording studio to create phantasmagoric tone poems, and left the seven-inch (17.5-cm) single in the dust as a medium for pop music. *The White Album* (1968) incorporated a dizzying panoply of styles into rock and roll that otherwise would have seemed utterly incongruous, and *Abbey Road* (1970) exuded a confident mastery that represents the apex of their development.

Long before the Beatles had demonstrated their inclination toward innovation, though, they had paved the way for other British groups. Their only real competition came from the Rolling Stones.

The Rolling Stones

London, home of the Rolling Stones, was in the midst of a full-scale blues revival when the Beatles hit. Whereas the Liverpool band maintained a typically British sense of reserve, peppering its repertoire with easy-listening fodder such as "Till There Was You" (1964), the Stones strove for down-and-dirty R&B authenticity. The song lists on their early records read like a "best of" from the heyday of Chicago blues, including classics by Chuck Berry, Muddy Waters, Bo Diddley, and Willie Dixon.

But after a disastrously underattended North American tour in 1964, it was clear that the American public wasn't going for it. Elvis had already done the job, and frontman Mick Jagger, for all his prancing and pouting, didn't cut the mustard.

To set themselves apart more decisively, the Rolling Stones transformed themselves into the dark underside of the Beatles "mop-top" image. Whereas the Fab Four insisted that they were "Happy Just to Dance With You," the Stones implored female fans with come-ons like "Let's

Spend the Night Together." They stopped smiling at photo sessions, and pioneered the snotty attitude that earned their punk-rock progeny at the close of the seventies so much opprobrium (and profit).

The gambit worked. Their first appearance on *The Ed Sullivan Show* prompted the venerable host to vow never to allow them back on the show. Naturally, they joined Sullivan on two more occasions. The Stones could not be ignored.

As their popularity grew, Jagger and guitarist Keith Richards developed into a crack songwriting team. One story has it that they began writing together after Lennon and McCartney cranked out "I Wanna Be Your Man" (1963) for them in twenty minutes between sets. Progressing from the anthemic "(I Can't Get No) Satisfaction" (1965) to "Street Fighting Man" and "Jumpin' Jack Flash" (both 1968), the Stones forged a hard-rock style that was firmly rooted in R&B, but distinctly their own. Their nonstop hits and extensive tours, coupled with Jagger's charisma and showmanship, has earned them the title, "World's Greatest Rock and Roll Band."

The Rolling Stones.

The Stones' enormous popularity—not to mention productivity, longevity, and consistency—has continued into the nineties, surviving changes in fashion, successful solo projects by just about all of the band's members, and several abortive break-ups. In their wake, they've left a remarkable catalog of rock and roll classics: "Brown Sugar" (1971), "Tumbling Dice" (1972), "It's Only Rock and Roll" (1974), "Beast of Burden" (1978), "Start Me Up" (1981), "Undercover of the Night" (1983), "Harlem Shuffle" (1986), and scores more. Their 1989 offering, *Steel Wheels,* appears in *Rolling Stone* magazine's list of *The 100 Greatest Albums of the Eighties.*

The Who

Riots broke out in Britain during the spring of 1964. They involved rival gangs of disaffected teenagers, as many as 1,500 scrappers in a single brawl. The gangs divided into two groups, Mods and Rockers. Rockers dressed in black leather and believed that good music began and ended with Elvis. Mods wore Italian shoes and short hair, affecting an air of class. Their brand of rock and roll was played by the Who.

In a savvy move on the part of their management, the Who were deliberately packaged to appeal to Mods. "My Generation" (1965) summed up the Mod spirit and defined the Who's sound through Roger Daltrey's deliberately stuttered verses, bass player John Entwistle's buzzing solos, and guitarist Pete Townshend's power chords. Townshend's famous motto from the song expresses the brash nihilism of the band's following, and a sentiment that the band couldn't possibly live down: "I hope I die before I get old."

Later releases found the group both more adventurous and more reflective, and Townshend came to the fore as an influential guitarist and, along with Lou Reed, one of the great rock and roll philosophers. Townshend offered quirky story lines and a razor-sharp sense of irony in hits such as "I'm a Boy" (1966) and "Pictures of Lily" (1967), as well as pop gems such as "The Kids Are All Right" (1966).

Meanwhile, the group's stage presentations gained a reputation as the most violent in rock and roll. Daltrey marched around the stage twirling his microphone overhead by its cable while Townshend slashed at his guitar, his arm swinging like a windmill. As a climax, Townshend splintered the guitar into tiny pieces and drummer Keith Moon smashed his entire kit. (Moon had been asked to become a member after joining the band onstage and pounding his foot right through the bass drum of their regular drummer.)

In 1969, the group booked a ground-breaking tour of European opera halls in order to debut *Tommy,* the first "rock opera." But despite their early dedication to the glories of youth, the Who pounded out undistinguished hits throughout the seventies, prompting the punks toward the end of the decade to single them out as the worst example of the music industry's isolation from its target audience. Such accusations only gained credence in 1979, when eleven Who fans were crushed to death in a stampede for seats at a poorly organized concert.

Even the untimely demise of Keith Moon, who died of a drug overdose in 1978, did not stop them. In 1982, the band finally called it a day. Townshend and Daltrey continue to record occasionally as solo artists.

© Wide World Photos

Smashing guitars and drum kits to pieces, the Who gained a reputation as the most violently energetic performers in rock and roll.

The American Defense

In garages across the world, a generation of teenagers, inspired by the Beatles, the Stones, the Who, and other British Invaders, picked up electric guitars. In America, the response amounted to an outburst of activity in various regional scenes during 1964 and 1966, most notably the beginnings of folk rock in Los Angeles and the psychedelic underground in San Francisco. In at least one case, that of producer and one-man-band Todd Rundgren, the Invasion sparked a major talent. (Rundgren's first album with his Anglophilic band, the Nazz, came out in 1968; his first solo hit, "We Gotta Get You a Woman," in 1970.)

As the American record industry scrambled to regain lost sales, regional acts broke nationally, and a rash of mop-topped popsters vied with the Brits for Number One. An abbreviated Who's Who includes: Dino, Dezi & Billy (featuring Dezi Arnaz, Jr.), Tommy James & the Shondells ("I Think We're Alone Now"), Neil Diamond ("Cherry, Cherry"), Paul Revere & the Raiders ("Hungry"), the Guess Who (the militantly Canadian group that would become Bachman-Turner Overdrive during the seventies), the McCoys ("Hang on Sloopy"), the Young Rascals ("Groovin'"), the Association ("Along Comes Mary"), the Turtles (led by Howard Kaylan and Mark Volman, a.k.a. Flo & Eddie, who later joined Frank Zappa's Mothers of Invention), and everybody's favorites, the Monkees. Other nations got into the act as well, including Australia, with the Easybeats (younger brothers of whom eventually formed AC/DC).

Within a few years, this youthful energy—or at least those teen buyers whom it motivated—would be channeled into bubblegum rock. Spurred by the success of the Monkees, television executives created the Archies, a Saturday morning cartoon creation aimed squarely at a prepubescent audience. Real live musicians took the cue, resulting in "Simon Says" (1968) by the 1910 Fruitgum Company and a string of gastronomic hits, beginning with "Yummy, Yummy, Yummy" (1968), by the Ohio Express. In later years, artists such as Tiffany, New Kids on the Block, and the Teenage Mutant Ninja Turtles would continue the bubblegum tradition.

The American Defense was armed mostly with hard-edged pop. But amidst the dogged pursuit of craftsmanship, a few remarkably unpolished performances broke through, deliriously raw three-chord rock and roll bashed out by unschooled, but inspired, teenagers. The classic in this genre is the all-but-indecipherable "Louie, Louie" by the Kingsmen, but there were many others: "Wild Thing" by the Troggs, "96 Tears" by ?Question Mark & the Mysterians, "Pushin' Too Hard" by the Seeds, to name a few.

These mere blips on the rock and roll screen were the expressions of white teenagers who weren't ready for the big time, but didn't see why that should stop them; rough-and-ready antidotes to the scrubbing that even the Rolling Stones got on their way across the ocean. Virtually ignored at the time, they take on a lustre of historical importance in hindsight, for these records are the first inklings of the punk revolution that would ambush an unsuspecting public one decade later.

Meanwhile, the next musical moment was bubbling up not on the far-off shores of Britain, but out of the rich soil of America's own folk tradition.

Michael Ochs Archives

Thousands of U.S. bands formed in the wake of the British Invasion, among them the Association, whose sophisticated musical arrangements are among the high points of the American Defense.

Chapter Two

Special Interest Groups

THE TIMES THEY ARE A-CHANGIN':
FOLK ROCK

O n September 11, 1961, a wiry, wild-eyed man with an acoustic guitar stepped onto the stage of a small club in New York City for the first time, and became a major influence in the music of the next two decades. In a raspy, nasal voice, talking the notes he wasn't able to sing, Bob Dylan performed with an intensity and conviction that turned him into a legend virtually overnight.

The heart of Dylan's repertoire consisted of stark reworkings of traditional Appalachian ballads. But he was also a prolific songwriter, turning out his own vitriolic compositions that decried apathy, racism, warmongering, and other ills of modern society. His energy galvanized musicians on the folk circuit, mostly apostles of late-fifties traditionalists like Doc Watson, their black counterparts such as Sonny Terry and Brownie McGhee, and radical-liberal protest singers in the Pete Seeger mold. Adopting Dylan's posture of social relevance as well as his songs, folkies such as Joan Baez and Peter, Paul & Mary both updated and commercialized the folk tradition.

As Dylan's influence melded with that of the British Invasion, younger players formed the classic folk-rock bands. Less than a year after "I Want to Hold Your Hand," the Byrds opened the floodgates with a Dylan cover, "Mr. Tambourine Man" (1965). Next came the Lovin' Spoonful ("Do You Believe in Magic?"), Simon & Garfunkel ("The Sound of Silence"), Donovan ("Catch the Wind"), the Mamas & the Papas ("California Dreamin'"), and folk-pop *poseurs* Sonny & Cher ("I Got You Babe"). The Band, a Canadian group that backed Dylan well into the seventies, created some of that decade's best folk-inflected roots rock.

U.K. Folk Rock

In the United Kingdom, folk rockers mined the rich lodes of English, Irish, and Scottish traditional music. Groups such as Fairport Convention, Steeleye Span, and the more adventurous Traffic (featuring Steve Winwood) developed the British branch of folk rock. British folk rock continues today with the music of the unjustifiably obscure Richard Thompson and Ireland's premier folkpunk exponents, the Pogues. Meanwhile, Marxist folkie Billy Bragg sings American-style protest songs with an electric guitar and a British working-class accent.

Bob Dylan

The portentous 1961 debut of Bob Dylan represents the root of folk rock; at that time it was still pure folk. Dylan was born Robert Allen Zimmerman in 1941 in Hibbing, Minnesota. During his college years at the University of Minnesota, he adopted Dylan as a stage name in honor of the infamous Welsh poet Dylan Thomas. By the time he was a teenager, he had been through a variety of heroes from Marlon Brando to Hank Williams to Little Richard. In high school he settled on itinerant folksinger Woodie Guthrie. Guthrie's tradition dates back to the turn of the century, when the first battles were fought between industrial capitalists and the nascent trade unions. (Guthrie's life was depicted in the film *Bound for Glory*.)

Above: Legendary folksinger Pete Seeger. Opposite: The young Bob Dylan before his rebirth as the avatar of folk rock.

Michael Ochs Archives

The Byrds

In 1965, Dylan stood tall as one of the two major forces in white popular music; the other was the Beatles. The Byrds incorporated equal parts of both, and in time grew to encompass country influences as well.

Chicago-born guitarist Roger McGuinn took up the electric twelve-string after hearing the Beatles' *A Hard Day's Night* (1964), which features the instrument prominently. He formed the Byrds with a gifted young folkie named David Crosby (later of Crosby, Stills, Nash & Young), and their first single struck gold. "Mr. Tambourine Man" (1965) set the tone for a string of mid-sixties hits, including "Turn! Turn! Turn!" (1965) and "So You Wanna Be a Rock and Roll Star" (1967). "Eight Miles High" (1966), with its stunning John Coltrane-inspired guitar lead, was banned from airplay for supposed drug references. The band insisted that it describes an airplane flight.

In the wake of such successes, however, McGuinn grew restless. Pursuing artistic aims ever more abstract, he initiated a series of personnel changes, none of which measured up to the group's initial lineup. (The exception is 1968's *Sweetheart of the Rodeo,* the seminal country rock album.) Although they were extraordinarily popular in their day, the extent of the Byrds' influence became apparent only in the mid-eighties, when groups such as R.E.M. cited them as primary influences. It's worth noting that Tom Petty, virtually a McGuinn sound-alike, now plays with Dylan in the Traveling Wilburys.

Meanwhile, Dylan's stature—like that of a select few rock and roll pioneers—seems to grow every year. The confessional singer/songwriter movement of James Taylor and Joni Mitchell, which dominated the seventies, clearly reflected Dylan's influence. Since then, folk rock has waxed and waned; the most recent revival ignited the careers of artists such as 10,000 Maniacs and Canada's Cowboy Junkies.

Early Dylan songs such as "Blowin' in the Wind" (1963) and "The Times They Are a-Changin'" (1964) spoke in simple language and striking images of the failed ideals of post-war America, combining moral urgency and heavy doses of irony and wit with a hint of thermonuclear apocalypse. Both the form and the content were perfectly suited to a generation of college students who were beginning to march in the streets to the strains of "We Shall Overcome." Although his first album didn't sell well, Dylan acquired a cult following that grew steadily over the next few years.

In a curious reversal of the Rolling Stones, he refused to appear on *The Ed Sullivan Show* in 1963 after CBS forbade him to sing the politically charged "Talkin' John Birch Society Blues." However, after his third album in 1964, Dylan suddenly renounced political songwriting in favor of more personal concerns. "I want to write what's inside me," he said, and went about laying the groundwork for the confessional brand of singer/songwriters that would dominate the early seventies.

Along with politics, Dylan renounced the folksinger tradition. Donning an electric guitar before the stunned audience at the 1965 Newport Folk Festival, Dylan tore into "Maggie's Farm," backed by the Paul Butterfield Blues Band. Caustic, prophetic, and blues-based, the new sound was directly inspired by the British Invasion and its R&B precursors. The next three albums—*Bringing It All Back Home* (1965), *Highway 61 Revisited* (1965), and *Blonde on Blonde* (1966)—turned Dylan into a rock and roll superstar.

Dylan's newfound voice was silenced momentarily after a motorcycle crash in 1966 that left him with a broken neck. To the ears of many fans and critics, he never fully recovered. Dylan was only twenty-five years old, with many albums, some mediocre and some exceptional, still to come. Yet, even by that age, he had already spawned one of the great movements in rock and roll.

Paul Caruso Collection

Above: Melding Dylan and the Beatles, the Byrds developed a distinctive sound. Opposite: The late Jimi Hendrix still reigns as rock's most influential guitar virtuoso.

CROSSROADS:
THE LONDON BLUES REVIVAL AND BLUES ROCK

Lots of young people now feel they're not getting a fair deal. So they revert to something loud, harsh, almost verging on violence. If they didn't go to a concert, they might be going to a riot.

Jimi Hendrix, 1968

The advance guard of the British Invasion had been manned by English teenagers hooked on the American music of the previous decade. But they were only a part of the British music equation. The Rolling Stones, in fact, were the most successful, although most pop-oriented, of the London bands that played sped-up, flashed-out Chicago blues.

Unlike the Stones, however, the hardcore denizens of London's blues revival were far more dedicated to the style itself than to stardom. Given to flights of high-voltage guitar pyrotechnics and free-form jamming, British blues rock in its classic form was certainly blues, but it was blues for a modern age —an age in which men walked on the moon and made war on the soil of their third-world neighbors.

The British and North American Scenes

The London scene was a melange of some two dozen bands, most prominently Alexis Korner's Blues Incorporated (formed in 1962) and John Mayall's Bluesbreakers (beginning in 1963). The combined membership of those two bands included founders of virtually every important British Invasion and post-Invasion band. Cream and Led Zeppelin were their most illustrious offspring,

as well as the Yardbirds (enormously influential in their blending of raw blues and British pop), the Animals, Fleetwood Mac, Rod Stewart's Faces, Ten Years After, and the Nice.

As if by some secret agreement of global youth culture, blues rockers sprang up simultaneously across the Atlantic. The American scene gathered around Chicago guitarist and pianist Mike Bloomfield, an anomaly at the time insofar as he was a white kid who dedicated himself to the blues. With soulmate and harmonica player Paul Butterfield, he nurtured a small movement that included the Butterfield Blues Band, the Electric Flag, Canned Heat, and the Blues Project (led by Blood, Sweat & Tears founder Al Kooper).

Blues rock also flourished in Texas due to the ample talents of brothers Johnny and Edgar Winter. Stalwarts such as the late, great Stevie Ray Vaughn and perennial chart-toppers ZZ Top have kept Lone Star blues rock alive. Some Texans, such as Janis Joplin and Steve Miller (a pop sensation throughout the late seventies and early eighties),

moved to San Francisco to merge with the budding psychedelic scene.

But the greatest blues rocker—or more accurately, the greatest instrumentalist to emerge from rock and roll to this day—was a black man from Seattle, Washington. His name was James Marshall Hendrix.

Jimi Hendrix

Unlike many of rock and roll's greatest performers, particularly those of African ancestry, Jimi Hendrix grew up in middle-class surroundings. He joined the Army in 1959 at age seventeen, and upon his discharge began playing guitar on tour with Little Richard, Wilson Pickett, and the Isley Brothers. Hendrix, left-handed, played his guitar upside down (unlike fellow southpaw Paul McCartney, who had his bass restrung.)

© LDE/Archive Photos

Paul Caruso Collection

Paul Caruso Collection

Meanwhile, he released a series of albums that fused the psychedelic whimsy of the Beatles' *Sgt. Pepper* with electrifying blues. *Are You Experienced?* and *Axis: Bold as Love* (both 1967), collections of tightly knit rock arrangements, feature extensive use of studio effects and lyrics emphasizing consciousness expansion. *Electric Ladyland* (1968), its banned softcore cover featuring the bare breasts of a dozen fans, abandoned the pop-song format for meandering improvisational jams that gave Hendrix's guitar acrobatics free reign.

Nonetheless, Hendrix seemed dissatisfied with both his psychedelicized productions and his rock-idol image. Throughout 1969, he experimented with a variety of lineups that emphasized a more blues-based approach, but eventually he re-formed the Experience. Arrested at Toronto Airport in May 1969 for possession of heroin, Hendrix was acquitted when he explained that a fan dropped the drug into his suitcase. Meanwhile, his shows were marked by inconsistent musicianship and erratic behavior. In the middle of a 1970 performance at Madison Square Garden, he suddenly walked off of the stage.

Jimi Hendrix's tragically short period of creative genius came to an end on September 18, 1970, when he was found dead of vomit inhalation following an overdose of barbiturates. The coroner's report neither confirmed nor ruled out the possibility that his death was a suicide.

Cream and Eric Clapton

Hendrix's arrival in London had been amply prepared for by Cream. Between 1966 and 1968, they achieved the classic blend of blues-derived expressiveness and rock and roll aggression. Along the way, they pioneered the power-trio format (guitar, bass, drums) later adopted by Hendrix, and served as the launching pad for prototypical guitar hero, Eric Clapton.

Buttressed by drummer Ginger Baker and bass player Jack Bruce, Clapton jacked up to a deafening volume of classics by blues legends Muddy Waters ("Rollin' and Tumblin'"), Howlin' Wolf ("Spoon-

Initially, Hendrix was shy about fronting his own band. He began playing under his own name in early 1966, reasoning that if Bob Dylan could make it on the strength of his voice, then so could he.

But it was his guitar playing that truly set Hendrix apart. He was the first musician to use the electric guitar as an instrument on its own terms, rather than as an extension of the acoustic guitar. In his hands, it became a kamikaze dive-bomber screaming toward its target, a banshee wailing in agony, a siren singing irresistible melodies of apocalypse. His stage moves were equally dazzling; he plucked his guitar with his teeth, played

it behind his head, battered it, made love to it, and as a climactic set-closer, set it on fire.

At the suggestion of his manager, Hendrix began his solo career in Britain. Performances with his ruffle-clad interracial band, the Experience, made waves among Britain's rock aristocracy. With only one single to his credit, "Hey Joe," Hendrix scheduled his American debut at the 1967 Monterey Pop Festival. Success in America was immediate and unquestionable. In a historic mismatch, Hendrix then toured the States opening for television's pop confection, the Monkees. He backed out after a few nights of being booed off the stage.

ful"), and Robert Johnson ("Crossroads"). In live performance, this material metamorphosed into ponderous jams that highlighted Clapton's extraordinarily fluid and articulate guitar playing. He went on to make one of rock and roll's most passionate statements, "Layla" (1971), a tribute to his affair with Beatle George Harrison's then-wife (now a former wife of Clapton himself), and achieved massive commercial success during the mid-seventies.

Like other blues-rock pioneers, in the studio Cream opted for concise pop tunes such as "Sunshine of Your Love," "White Room," and "Badge" (all 1968). (The latter was co-composed by Clapton and George Harrison; the title came from Clapton's misreading of the lyric sheet, where Harrison had noted the middle section or "bridge.") Cream's arrangements, marked by thunderous unison lines of guitar and bass over a pile-driving backbeat, laid the foundation for blues rock's apotheosis in the form of Led Zeppelin.

Led Zeppelin

For high volume, monolithic riffing, and sheer sensory overload, Led Zeppelin remains unsurpassed. By 1968 ex-Yardbird Jimmy Page had contributed as a session guitarist to the Kinks' "You Really Got Me" (the prophetic 1964 protometal classic, later covered by both Van Halen and Brian Eno's 801 band), the Who's "I Can't Explain" (1965), Joe Cocker's "With a Little Help From My Friends" (1968), and "Gloria" (1966) by Them, featuring the young Van Morrison. During sessions for Donovan's *Hurdy Gurdy Man* in 1968, he met bass player John Paul Jones. With the addition of the fleet-footed John Bonham on drums and raw-voiced belter Robert Plant, a supergroup was born.

Page, one of the great guitarists of the era—less lyrical than Clapton, less flamboyant than Hendrix, but more concise than either—had taken over the bass position in the Yardbirds in 1966, soon sharing lead guitar with the equally formidable Jeff Beck. (The two recorded only two songs together, "Happenings Ten Years Time Ago" and "Psycho Daisies," both with Page on bass.) When that band disintegrated, Page toured Europe with Jones, Bonham, and Plant as the New Yardbirds.

In late 1968, they adopted the name by which they would become world famous. "Led Zeppelin" was actually a joke, a jibe from the Who's John Entwistle that the band would go over like the world's biggest lead balloon.

Unlike the more hit-oriented Yardbirds, Led Zeppelin's approach was initially pure blues rock, right down to compositions such as "The Lemon Song" (1969), credited to the band, that they stole wholesale from Chicago bluesmen. By *Led Zeppelin III* (1970), their sound had evolved into a careful balance of acoustic and electric elements, and for the fourth edition, they incorporated the kind of ersatz mystical imagery, appropriated from Celtic mythology, that has since become *de rigueur* in heavy metal.

The monumental "Stairway to Heaven" (1971), by far their most popular song—although it was never released as a single—established Led Zeppelin as both an artistic and a commercial behemoth. Subsequent tours set records for attendance throughout the world, usually breaking precedents set years before by the Beatles. They continued to rack up hits until John Bonham's untimely death in 1980. Yet another tragic example of rock and roll excess, the drummer died after downing forty shots of vodka in twelve hours. To this day, Led Zeppelin is Atlantic Records' best-selling act.

Consistently lambasted by critics throughout their heyday, Led Zeppelin is now recognized as one of the major influences on the music of the eighties and nineties. Their records display a remarkable range of imagination and ingenuity, and their style is among the most imitated in rock. Top-Forty hard rockers strain to match Robert Plant's inflections, Zep riffs abound in the sampled collages of rap, and virtually the entire genre of heavy metal owes its existence to them.

Metal, however, would require input from bands less dedicated to the blues. At the dawn of the seventies, this hypercharged blend of blues riffs and teen fantasy had earned little more than a cult following (not to mention the universal condemnation of critics). Nonetheless, as Iron Butterfly demonstrated in 1968 with the cryptic "Ina-Gadda-Da-Vida," the seeds had taken root. Soon the mutant strain would grow into one of the major branches of rock's family tree.

© Brian McLaughlin/Michael Ochs Archives

Opposite: Led Zeppelin built the bridge between the blues and heavy metal, emerging as one of the primary influences on rock and roll in the 1990s. Above: A guitarist of exceptional fluidity and lyricism, bluesman Eric Clapton was the first certified "guitar hero" of rock and roll.

BREAK ON THROUGH TO THE OTHER SIDE:

PSYCHEDELIA

Earsplitting as they were, Cream and Jimi Hendrix were being edged off the charts in 1967 by even more disturbing newcomers. In an obvious drug reference, the Jefferson Airplane's Grace Slick implored fans to "feed your head" in "White Rabbit." Meanwhile, Jim Morrison, leader of the Doors, evoked the Oedipal drama in his song "The End." "Father," he stated with utmost calm, "I want to kill you. Mother, I want to—" Morrison completed the thought with an agonized scream. Clearly, popular music had become infected by a force more alien than either African-American blues or British working-class desperation.

That force was the mind-altering power of psychedelic drugs, particularly LSD. Its purveyors were a neo-tribal aggregation of cultural revolutionaries known as hippies, and it spread from an epicenter marked by August Owsley Stanley III's infamous drug laboratory in San Francisco.

Hippies were spiritual children of the Beats, a group of poets and authors who came to San Francisco to escape the spiritual morbidity of American life in the early fifties. Unlike the Beats though, hippies celebrated life in a joyous, extroverted, inclusive way. They pioneered the flamboyant clothing, communal lifestyle, political awareness, and mass meetings—the origin of such gargantuan rock festivals as Woodstock—that came to express the rebellious optimism of the nation's youth at the close of the sixties.

The Haight-Ashbury district was the center of hippie life, and between 1965 and 1968 housed over a thousand bands. They had incomprehensible names such as the Jefferson Airplane, the Grateful Dead, Big Brother & the Holding Company (which featured Janis Joplin), and Moby Grape. To an urbanized brew of folk and blues they added a propensity for static droning in the manner of the Indian *raga,* feedback harnessed as a musical element rather than as an accidental annoyance, lengthy free-form jamming, and rear-projection light shows in which liquid images melted and converged. Psychedelic performances emphasized the interaction among musicians and audience rather than focusing on a charismatic star. Often they were free of charge, more community ritual than entertainment.

Above all, the San Francisco underground imbued rock and roll with a new sense of purpose. No longer was it a way of avoiding a "straight job," a way to have a good time, an homage to childhood heroes, or even a means of self-expression. The purpose of psychedelic music was to incite a full-scale cultural revolution, the overthrow of the "establishment" in favor of a society based on "free minds, free bodies, free dope, and free music," to quote Paul Kantner, leader of the scene's flagship band, the Jefferson Airplane.

The Jefferson Airplane

The Airplane formed in 1965 when Marty Balin, inspired by Bob Dylan's early performances in New York, returned to the West Coast in search of collaborators. (The group's name arose as a joke, the name of bluesman Blind Lemon Jefferson evolving into Blind Jefferson Airplane. "Airplane" was often used to refer to a roach clip.) After a few personnel changes, the lineup solidified around guitarists Paul Kantner and Jorma Kaukonen and bass player Jack Casady. With the addition of ex-model Grace Slick, the extroverted daughter of an investment banker, the Jefferson Airplane took off. A contract with RCA made them the first San Francisco band to hit the big time.

The group's folk-based sound incorporated a fascination with drugs and revolutionary ideals to produce the psychedelic classic *Surrealistic Pillow* (1966), including their biggest hit "Somebody to Love." Personnel problems plagued the band, though, as Balin left to clear his head and Kaukonen and Casady to form Hot Tuna. In 1970, Kantner and Slick, now husband and wife, used the name Jefferson Starship for an obscure but engaging album, *Blows Against the Empire,* featuring cameos by virtually every important figure on the West Coast music scene.

For Balin's return in 1974, the Airplane completed its metamorphosis into the Jefferson Starship. Amazingly, the group consistently topped the charts well into the eighties, serving up unabashedly nonrevolutionary fare such as "Miracles" (1975), "Count on Me" (1978), and "We Built This City on Rock and Roll" (1985). The Airplane/Starship's longevity, though, is nothing compared with that of their Bay Area siblings, the Grateful Dead.

The Grateful Dead

The Dead eventually settled in 1966 out of the incessant accretion and fragmentation of numerous Haight-Ashbury folk and blues bands. Serving as the house band for the Merry Pranksters' legendary Acid Tests (in which huge numbers of people would drink spiked "electric Kool Aid" and freak out together), the band stabilized around guitarist and guiding light Jerry Garcia. The classic lineup included guitarist Bob Weir, Phil Lesh on bass, keyboard player Pigpen McKernan, and drummers Bill Kreutzmann and Mickey Hart. The Dead also earned a reputation for playing three-to-five-hour sets during which virtually anything might happen (in contrast with the Beatles' usual twenty minutes of three-minute tunes), and to this day they remain the ultimate hippie band.

The Dead's first few albums defined psychedelia, San Francisco style, but failed to expand their cult following. Meanwhile, they switched to a more earthy folk flavor for *Workingman's Dead* and *American Beauty* (both 1970), ushering in the band's most productive period. Great originals from this period including "Uncle John's Band," "Truckin'," "U.S. Blues," "Sugar Magnolia," and "Casey Jones." Touring incessantly, they picked up new fans at every stop and churned out numerous

live albums, while continuing to experiment with the form and content of their music in landmarks *Blues For Allah* (1975), *Terrapin Station* (1977), *Reckoning* (1981), and *In the Dark* (1987).

Grateful Dead fans, known as "Deadheads," are distinguished by a level of loyalty unmatched in popular music. Years may go by without a new release, but Deadheads, now a generation removed from the band's San Francisco heyday, still camp out in front of the ticket outlets days ahead of scheduled concert appearances. In sharp contrast with every other band in the industry, the Dead encourage amateur taping of their concerts, and recorded shows are featured weekly in a syndicated radio show. If the San Francisco scene failed to change American society at large, the Grateful Dead have maintained their own little island of eternal hippiedom within the belly of the beast.

Paul Caruso Collection

The Doors

The Doors differed from the other West Coast bands in that they hailed from Los Angeles, home of Hollywood, surfing, and the Monkees. When front man Jim Morrison exhorted his audience to "break on through to the other side," he invoked the same revolutionary tendency as his compatriots to the north. But he channeled it in a different direction, one inspired by the aloof pessimism of the Beat poets. The Doors represented the dark side of the hippies' flower-power rhetoric, the repressed urges that soon would explode into the horrors of My Lai and the Manson family.

Taking their name from Aldous Huxley's psychedelic handbook, *The Doors of Perception* (via a poem by William Blake), the Doors made their first album soon after the band's inception in 1967. It

© Jason Lauré

Left: The Doors, featuring the charismatic and self-destructive poet Jim Morrison, presented a dark vision of psychedelia. Page 48: Pink Floyd.

Michael Ochs Archives

conceptual coherence and studio production, *Dark Side of the Moon* (1973). Artistic success didn't interfere with commercial appeal, as *Moon* occupied the the Billboard charts for a record 700 consecutive weeks—well over a decade.

The Death and Rebirth of Psychedelia

By the late sixties, however, the psychedelic revolution was fading. After a triumphant global coming-out at the Woodstock festival in 1969, the movement's spirit was dealt an incapacitating blow only months later when members from the Hell's Angels knifed a fan to death at the Rolling Stones' free Altamont Raceway concert. During a protest of President Nixon's bombing of Cambodia at Kent State University, Ohio, on May 8, 1970, National Guardsmen shot to death four students. By October, Jim Morrison, Jimi Hendrix, and Janis Joplin were all dead, and naïve optimism was no longer a tenable posture for young Americans to assume. Escape into Top Forty musical blandness was once again the next best thing.

The visionary thrust of the psychedelic movement eventually became the basis for the progressive rock bands of the seventies, while its coloristic bent contributed to the punked-up art rock of such groups as Roxy Music and Talking Heads. Throughout the years, the psychedelic style (if not its substance) has seen periodic revivals by such groups as the Dukes of Stratosphere (actually XTC in disguise), Echo & the Bunnymen, Teardrop Explodes, Three O'Clock, Green on Red, and more recently by Lenny Kravitz and Stone Roses.

remains one of the most dramatic documents of the era, featuring "The End," "Break on Through," and the classic "Light My Fire." Further albums yielded the haunting "People Are Strange" (1967), "Hello, I Love You" (1968, which prompted a successful plagiarism suit by the Kinks' Ray Davies, author of "All Day and All of the Night"), the exuberant "Touch Me" (1969), and the eerie "Riders on the Storm" (1971).

As the band's stature grew, Morrison's grandiosity and self-destructiveness became problematic (as dramatized in Oliver Stone's 1991 biopic, *The Doors*). Morrison was arrested on obscenity charges in late 1967, and for exposing himself on stage the following year. Slipping into depression and chronic alcoholism, he quit the band in order to concentrate on poetry (subsequently published in two volumes) and moved to Paris, France. Mysteriously, he was found dead of a heart attack at age 27 on July 3, 1971, although some claim that he is still alive. Morrison's grave at Père Lachaise Cemetery in France is among the most popular sights in Europe.

Pink Floyd

News of the psychedelic revolution reached Britain by word of mouth, and immediately Swinging London established its own acid scene. Rumor has it that Pink Floyd's early music was based on oral reports of what was happening in the States, rather than direct experience with the scene itself. (Let it be said, however, that the band, originally called the Screaming Abdabs, was founded by Syd Barrett in 1964.)

Named for obscure American bluesmen Pink Anderson and Floyd Council, the group recorded their first album, *Piper at the Gates of Dawn,* in 1967. The album surrounded screwball pop songs by Barrett ("Arnold Layne" is about a kleptomaniac transvestite who pilfers ladies' underwear) with longer group improvisations that showcased an unusually open-ended approach to rock. The records that followed trace Pink Floyd's development into one of the most creative bands of the next two decades, culminating in their masterpiece of

Rock and Roll Heaven

Hope I die before I get old.

The Who, "My Generation," 1965

The Big Bopper: February 3, 1959, airplane crash
Buddy Holly: February 3, 1959, airplane crash
Ritchie Valens: February 3, 1959, airplane crash
Eddie Cochran: April 19, 1960, car crash
Johnny Burnette (Johnny Burnette & the Rock and Roll Trio): August 15, 1964, boating accident
Sam Cooke: December 11, 1964, gunshot
Bobby Fuller (the Bobby Fuller Four): July 18, 1966, asphyxiation
Otis Redding: December 10, 1967, airplane crash
Ronald Caldwell (the Bar-Kays): December 10, 1967, airplane crash
Carl Cunningham (the Bar-Kays): December 10, 1967, airplane crash
Phalon Jones (the Bar-Kays): December 10, 1967, airplane crash
James King (the Bar-Kays): December 10, 1967, airplane crash
Frankie Lymon (Frankie Lymon & the Teenagers): February 27, 1968, drug overdose
Brian Jones (the Rolling Stones): July 3, 1969, drowning
Tammi Terrell: March 16, 1970, brain tumor
Jimi Hendrix: September 18, 1970, drug overdose
Janis Joplin: October 3, 1970, drug overdose
Alan Wilson (Canned Heat): 1970, drug overdose
Jim Morrison (the Doors): July 3, 1971, heart attack
Donald McPherson (the Main Ingredient): July 4, 1971, leukemia
King Curtis: August 13, 1971, stabbing
Gene Vincent: October 12, 1971, ulcers
Duane Allman (the Allman Brothers): October 29, 1971, motorcycle crash
Clyde McPhatter (the Drifters): March 13, 1972, heart attack
Brian Cole (the Association): August 2, 1972, drug overdose
Berry Oakley (the Allman Brothers): November 11, 1972, motorcycle crash
Pigpen (the Grateful Dead): March 8, 1973, liver disease
Paul Williams (the Temptations): August 17, 1973, suicide
Jim Croce: September 20, 1973, airplane crash
Bobby Darin: December 20, 1973, heart failure
Mama Cass: July 29, 1974, choking

Robbie McIntosh (the Average White Band): September 23, 1974, drug overdose
Louis Jordan: February 4, 1975, heart attack
Peter Ham (Badfinger): April 23, 1975, suicide
Al Jackson (Booker T & the MGs): October 1, 1975, gunshot
Howlin' Wolf: January 10, 1976, kidney disease
Florence Ballard (the Supremes): February 22, 1976, cardiac arrest
Paul Kossoff (Free): March 18, 1976, heart attack
Keith Relf (the Yardbirds): May 14, 1976, electrocution
Tommy Bolin: December 4, 1976, drug overdose
Freddy King: December 28, 1976, ulcers
William Powell (the O'Jays): May 26, 1977, extended illness
Elvis Presley: August 16, 1977, heart failure
Marc Bolan (T. Rex): September 16, 1977, car crash
Ronnie Van Zant (Lynyrd Skynyrd): October 20, 1977, airplane crash
Steve Gaines (Lynyrd Skynyrd): October 20, 1977, airplane crash
Cassie Gaines (Lynyrd Skynyrd): October 20, 1977, airplane crash
Terry Kath (Chicago): January 23, 1978, self-inflicted gunshot
Keith Moon (the Who): September 7, 1978, drug overdose
Sid Vicious (the Sex Pistols): February 2, 1979, drug overdose
Van McCoy: July 6, 1979, heart attack
Minnie Riperton: July 12, 1979, cancer
Dorsey Burnette (Johnny Burnette & the Rock and Roll Trio): August 19, 1979, heart attack
Jimmy McCulloch (Wings), September 17, 1979, gunshot
Bon Scott (AC/DC): February 19, 1980, alcohol overdose
Jon Jon Paulus (the Buckinghams): March 26, 1980, drug overdose
Tommy Caldwell (the Marshall Tucker Band): April 28, 1980, car crash
Ian Curtis (Joy Division): May 1980, suicide
Keith Godchaux (the Grateful Dead): July 22, 1980, car crash
John Bonham (Led Zeppelin): September 25, 1980, alcohol overdose
John Lennon (the Beatles): December 8, 1980, gunshot
Bill Haley (Bill Haley & the Comets): February 9, 1981, heart attack
Bob Hite (Canned Heat): April 6, 1981, heart attack
Bob Marley (the Wailers): May 11, 1981, cancer
Rushton Moreve (Steppenwolf): July 1, 1981, car crash
Harry Chapin: July 16, 1981, car crash
Lightnin' Hopkins: January 30, 1982, natural causes

John Belushi (the Blues Brothers): March 5, 1982, drug overdose
Addie Harris (the Shirelles): June 10, 1982, heart attack
James Honeyman-Scott (the Pretenders): June 16, 1982, drug overdose
Bill Justis: July 16, 1982, natural causes
Joe Tex: August 13, 1982, heart attack
Karen Carpenter (the Carpenters): February 4, 1983, heart failure
Danny Rapp (Danny & the Juniors): April 4, 1983, gunshot
Pete Farndon (the Pretenders): April 14, 1983, drug overdose
Felix Pappalardi (the Rascals): April 17, 1983, gunshot
Muddy Waters: April 30, 1983, heart attack
Clarence E. Quick (the Del Vikings): May 5, 1983, heart attack
Dennis Wilson (the Beach Boys): December 28, 1983, drowning
Alexis Korner: January 1, 1984, cancer
Jackie Wilson: January 21, 1984, heart attack
Marvin Gaye: April 1, 1984, gunshot
Phillippe Wynne (the Spinners): July 13, 1984, heart attack
David Byron (Uriah Heep): February 29, 1985, unknown cause
Ricky Wilson (the B-52's): October 13, 1985, cancer
Big Joe Turner: November 24, 1985, kidney failure
Ian Stewart (sideman for the Rolling Stones): December 12, 1985, heart attack
Ricky Nelson: December 31, 1985, airplane crash
Phil Lynott (Thin Lizzy): January 4, 1986, drug overdose
Richard Manuel (the Band): March 4, 1986, suicide
O'Kelly Isley (the Isley Brothers): March 31, 1986, cerebral hemorrhage
Paul Butterfield (the Butterfield Blues Band): May 4, 1987, drug overdose
Peter Tosh: September 11, 1987, gunshot
Andy Gibb: March 10, 1988, heart ailment
Brook Benton: April 9, 1988, spinal meningitis
Dave Prater (Sam & Dave): April 9, 1988, car crash
Roy Buchanan: August 14, 1988, suicide
Roy Orbison: December 6, 1988, heart attack
Sylvester: December 16, 1988, AIDS
Cowboy (Grandmaster Flash & the Furious Five): September 8, 1989, drug overdose
Stevie Ray Vaughan: August 27, 1990, helicopter crash
Del Shannon: February 9, 1990, suicide
Steve Marriott (the Faces, Humble Pie): April 20, 1991, burns
Miles Davis: October 1991, pneumonia
Freddie Mercury (Queen): November 24, 1991, AIDS

BORN TO BE WILD:

HARD ROCK, GLITTER, AND THE BIRTH OF HEAVY METAL

The notion that rock and roll should be played hard and loud—the harder and louder, the better—was an idea fully realized in the thunderous unison riffs of blues rock. The notion that these qualities were essential to rock in all of its manifestations—even to the exclusion of melody, harmony, orchestration, or instrumental finesse—was the cornerstone of hard rock.

Certainly, the Who and the Rolling Stones had been moving in that direction for some time. Beginning with Steppenwolf's "Born to Be Wild" in the summer of 1968 (and simultaneously, "Jumpin' Jack Flash" by the Stones), rock became increasingly harder, louder, rawer, and rowdier, until it reached a pitch of jackhammer impact and steamroller momentum that could only be called heavy metal.

Hard Rock: Steppenwolf, Grand Funk Railroad, and Deep Purple

Steppenwolf, a Canadian group that relocated to the States (leader John Kay began as an East German who defected to Canada), was basically a very heavy pop band, as evidenced by "Born to Be Wild"'s immediate follow-ups, "Magic Carpet Ride" and "Rock Me." Their raw sound allied Steppenwolf with the legendary Detroit underground groups Iggy and the Stooges and the MC5. In hindsight, though, those bands were more a premonition of punk, descendants of the American Defense, than a harbinger of heavy metal.

Grand Funk Railroad

The consummate hard-rock band, Grand Funk Railroad debuted at the 1969 Atlanta Pop Festival before an audience of 100,000. Their reception was wildly enthusiastic, despite observations that the music was plodding and tuneless. Universally loathed by critics, the Michigan-based trio nonetheless achieved gold-record status with virtually every release. Their commercial breakthrough arrived in 1973, when "We're an American Band" reached the top of the charts.

Deep Purple

The British band Deep Purple, however, surely donned the leaden mantle of heaviest band in the world. Leaving behind the stylistic confusion of their early years, the group consolidated a hard-rock identity by 1973 that culminated in the blockbuster *Machine Head.* The album featured the stultifying "Smoke on the Water," which describes one of their gigs as the opening act for Frank Zappa during which the Montreux Casino burned down. Buoyed by an effective riff-refrain, "Smoke" became a staple of garage-band repertoire.

In terms of heavy metal in the nineties, Deep Purple circa 1973 are revered ancestors. Their proto-metal compatriots include Uriah Heep, Status Quo, Humble Pie, UFO, Nazareth, and Ted Nugent & the Amboy Dukes, Foghat, Mountain, and Montrose.

The Birth of Metal: Iron Butterfly

But metal already had been plodding toward recognition as a distinct style for nearly five years. In 1968, an obscure band called Iron Butterfly shocked the world with a seventeen-minute epic bearing the curious title "Ina-Gadda-Da-Vida." It has been said that the original title was "In the Garden of Eden." Vocalist Erik Braun had arrived at rehearsals not entirely sober, though, and the resulting garble was too good to waste. The seventeen-minute version was simply a pretake warm-up, but everyone agreed that it should be released in that form. (Patient listeners will note that organist Doug Ingle relies on "God Rest Ye Merry Gentlemen" to get him through his rather lengthy solo.)

Opposite: One of the heaviest of the hard rockers, the British band Deep Purple. Inset: Hard rockers Grand Funk Railroad overcame critical derision to capture the hearts of audiences during the early 1970s.

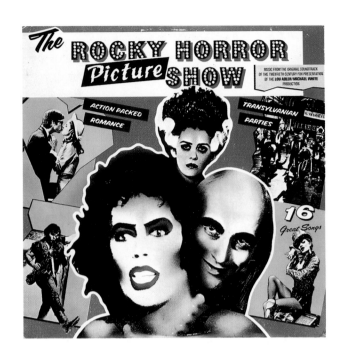

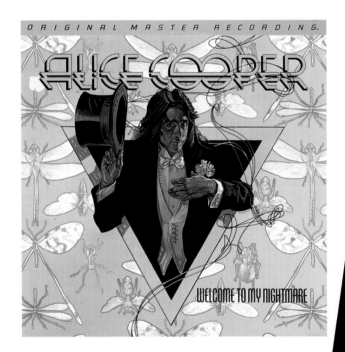

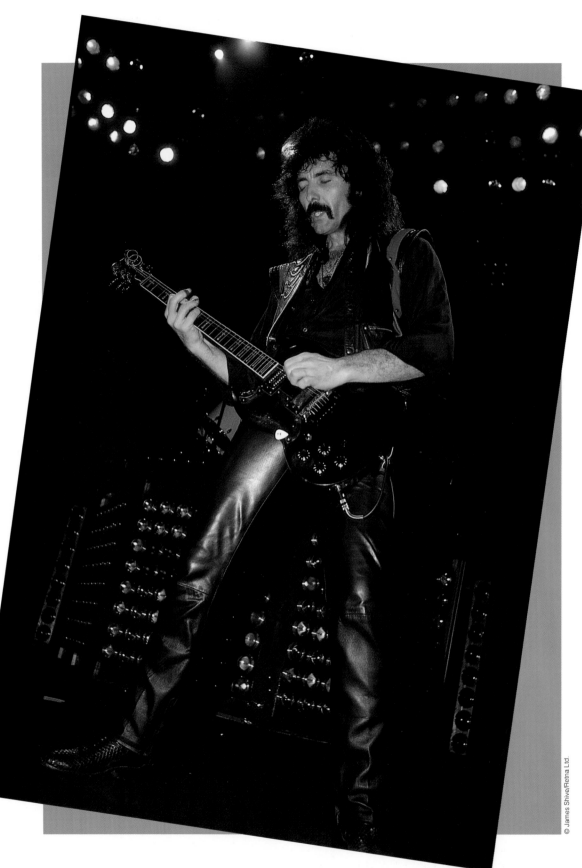

This page: Tony Iommi, formerly of Black Sabbath. Opposite:
David Bowie.

Black Sabbath

As if to negate the naïve optimism of the Woodstock generation, heavy metal proper burst out upon the world the following year with the release of Black Sabbath's eponymous 1970 debut. Led by John "Ozzy" Osbourne (the grand old man of metal, still performing in the early nineties), Sabbath set new standards of viciousness and overall bad vibes. The tempos were faster than much of blues rock, the riffs simpler, the vocals more strident, the lyrics even more despairing. Most important, the band's iconography reflected dark satanic themes; indeed, Ozzy made headlines by biting the heads off of live bats onstage.

Glitter Rock

While heavy metallurgists jumped into black leather, pentagram pendants, and other demonic garb, another fashion movement was afoot—glitter (also called glam). Glitter rock isn't associated with a specific musical style as much as a period of time, roughly between 1972 and 1975 when it reached a glorious apex in the cult film *The Rocky Horror Picture Show* (featuring the debut of Meatloaf). Glitter fashion sought to shock by departing from the tradition of rock and roll machismo established by Elvis in favor of makeup, cross dressing, and an overall smearing of the lines between the sexes.

Little Richard, with his lipstick and bouffant hairdo, had set the precedent in the late fifties. Since then, questions of sexual identity had been swept under the rock and roll rug (with rare exceptions: in 1966 the Stones appeared in drag on the sleeve for the single "Have You Seen Your Mother, Baby Standing in the Shadow?"). But in 1973, the previously macho Mick Jagger was prancing around onstage in pancake and eyeliner, while Elton John, once a sensitive schoolboy, was flaunting feather boas and bisexuality. At the same time, glitter united a num-

ber of lesser hard rockers into something resembling a movement, particularly Britain's T. Rex ("Bang a Gong," 1972), Mott the Hoople ("All the Young Dudes," 1972), and longrunning singles band Slade ("Cum on Feel the Noize," 1973).

Alice Cooper

Glitter found its way into the North American Top Forty on the coattails of a man called Alice. Born Vincent Furnier, Alice Cooper changed his name when a Ouija board revealed that he was the reincarnation of a witch. He began his recording career under the auspices of Frank Zappa. (Zappa's band, the Mothers of Invention, had built upon the twisted logic of their own name by appearing in drag on their album covers.) Decked out in a clinging dress and ghoulish makeup, a pet boa constrictor wrapped around his neck, Cooper brought his shows to a climax by offering his own neck to a guillotine.

His hits "Eighteen" and "School's Out" (both 1971) stand out as hard-rock radio classics.

David Bowie's Glitter Period

David Bowie, in the days before he defected to art rock and blue-eyed soul, took ambisexuality, outrageous fashion statements, and rock and roll theater to even greater heights. Decked out in a glittering space suit, high platform shoes, and spiked orange hair, Bowie descended to the stage in a space ship. During the early seventies, he wore his makeup and outlandish outfits offstage as well as on, and the physical androgyny of his face and body were paralleled in his celebrated bisexuality. Although his main musical contributions have been as an art rocker and as one of the world's premier purveyors of blue-eyed soul, Bowie was instrumental in glitterizing fellow hard rockers Mott the Hoople, Iggy Pop, and Lou Reed (whose 1973 hit "Walk on the Wild Side" boasted surprisingly overt references to transvestitism, drug abuse, and oral sex).

The New York Dolls

The most prophetic example of glitter style were the New York Dolls. Managed by marketing *wunderkind* Malcolm McLaren, who later created the Sex Pistols, the Dolls positively reeked of transsexuality. Aping Marilyn Monroe and Mae West, they struck languorous poses, showing off teased hair, halter tops, and hot pants. Behind their makeup, the Dolls—fronted by David Johansen (a.k.a. Buster Poindexter)—were tough, obnoxious, and streetwise. Likewise, the music was remarkably raw and confrontational for 1975. Out-of-control and nearly inept, it foreshadowed the punk movement that was already beginning to ferment in the clubs of New York and London.

Kiss

If the Dolls stood at the confluence between glitter and punk, Kiss met at the fork between glitter and metal. Working as a school teacher in New York City, Gene Simmons was aware of both the Dolls and Alice Cooper. Determined to go one step further, he put together a band in which each member adopted a comic-book persona: guitarist Paul Stanley as the glamour boy, lead guitarist Ace Frehley as alien from outer space, drummer Peter Criss as cutie-pie kitty cat, and Simmons himself as sex-crazed Kabuki monster.

It took over an hour to put on their makeup, but when they hit the stage, it was a frenzy of fire-eating, smoke bombs, hydraulic lifts, and other attention-getting devices designed to distinguish their otherwise undistinguished hard rock. To their credit, Kiss racked up one bona-fide teen-party classic, "Rock and Roll All Nite" (1975), and, amazingly, continued to sell platinum throughout the eighties. In the process, they spawned a Saturday morning cartoon show and two Marvel comic books.

© Arthur D'Amario III/FPG International

© Syndication International, Ltd.

Hard Pop

By 1973, various innovations of hard rock, metal, and glitter were finding their way into the mainstream. The first pop-metal bands, notably Aerosmith, prompted the emergence of a style that mixed hard rock with a lyricism, romanticism, and general pandering to the marketplace that had been absent when hard rockers fancied themselves some kind of an alternative. The result was a preponderance of derivative pop acts in rock and roll clothing such as Boston ("More Than a Feeling," 1976), Heart ("Magic Man," 1976), Foreigner ("Hot Blooded," 1978), Journey ("Don't Stop Believin'," 1981), Pat Benatar ("Hit Me With Your Best Shot," 1981), and even erstwhile psychedelics, the Jefferson Starship ("We Built This City," 1985).

Assimilating influences from British progressive rockers such as Yes, hard pop took on all of that genre's grandiose posture without retaining any of the daring and musical richness that made it interesting. (The progressives, in turn, learned from the hard poppers how to remain commercially viable in the eighties: witness Asia.) Representatives of this approach include the American groups Kansas ("Point of Know Return," 1977) and Styx ("Come Sail Away," 1977), and their superior British counterparts Queen ("We Are the Champions," 1978) and Supertramp ("Give a Little Bit," 1977). Rush and Triumph, both from Ontario, consistently topped the Canadian charts throughout the late seventies and the eighties, eventually developing considerable followings in the United States and the United Kingdom.

The hard pop bands made the best-selling records of the seventies. Their music, however, suggested that something had gone seriously wrong with rock and roll. The hits were bland, white-bread retreads of old ideas, shorn of rough edges, passionate delivery, or any hint of creative struggle. They were calculated to fuel FM radio (AOR, or album-oriented radio) and fill stadiums across America. They were promoted by the major labels to the exclusion of virtually everything else short of pure pop (disco was a grass-roots phenomenon, and didn't require promotion).

Indeed, the mid-seventies were the era of "corporate rock," and it was time for the kids to take back what truly belonged to them. And, as the seventies came to a close, the punks came along to do the dirty work.

SWEET HOME ALABAMA:
SOUTHERN BOOGIE

British musicians responded to the hardening of rock by fancying themselves in league with the Devil. In the United States, young southerners saw hard rock as a call to reclaim the rockabilly legacy that was rightfully theirs. The British Invasion, the Soul Explosion, and Nashville's sellout to country pop had robbed the Confederacy of rock and roll. To paraphrase the Rolling Stones, what could a poor (good old) boy do except play in a rock and roll band?

And throughout the seventies they did just that, playing a down-home style that came to be known as southern boogie. The genre's prototypes were the Allman Brothers and their acolytes, Lynyrd Skynyrd. Playing no-frills barroom rock and roll with dashes of blues and country, these southern rockers pushed a regional scene into the national spotlight. They opened the door for Wet Willie ("Keep on Smilin'," 1974), Elvin Bishop ("Fooled Around and Fell in Love," 1976), and the Atlanta Rhythm Section ("So Into You," 1977), not to mention progressive southerners Sea Level and the Dixie Dregs, and eighties' acts such as the Outlaws ("Riders in the Sky," 1980) and .38 Special ("Back Where You Belong," 1984). By then, though, southern boogie's most exciting time had long since passed. It really lasted only a few short years, during the Roman-candle career of Duane Allman.

The Allman Brothers Band

In 1969, brothers Duane and Gregg Allman would jam in Daytona Beach, Florida, with a loose group of guys that they called the Allman Brothers Band. Based on the blues, Chuck Berry, and the Beatles, the Allmans' sound was distinguished by Gregg's gospel-influenced organ, the precision dual guitar leads of Duane and Dicky Betts, and a powerhouse rhythm section that included two drummers. The group also injected a heavy dose of the kind of free-form improvisation that had been a hallmark of blues rock and psychedelia, and performed instrumentals in the manner of the surf groups.

The Allman Brothers' first two albums in 1969 and 1970 met with modest success. At the same time, Duane gained a reputation as a red-hot session player working for the likes of Wilson Pickett, Aretha Franklin, and King Curtis at Muscle Shoals Studio in Alabama. With their third effort, *The Allman Brothers Band at the Fillmore East* (1971), the Brothers broke nationally, selling gold almost immediately. The album also established Duane as one of the finest lead guitar players in North America. (His 1971 duet with Eric Clapton on Derek & the Dominoes' "Layla" is one of rock and roll's transcendent moments.)

But the Allman Brothers' rise came to a sudden, tragic halt when Duane was killed in a motorcycle accident the same year. One year later, bass player Berry Oakley perished in a similar crash. The band managed to regroup, scoring their first chart hit, "Ramblin' Man," in 1973, but they never managed to regain their former momentum. In the years since, Gregg Allman and Dicky Betts have pursued solo careers and the group has been through numerous breakups and comebacks, the latest in 1991. After the Allman Brothers Band, it was left to Lynyrd Skynyrd to continue the southern boogie tradition.

Lynyrd Skynyrd

Directly inspired by the Allmans, Lynyrd Skynyrd formed in Jacksonville, Florida, out of the long-standing friendship between singer Ronnie Van Zant and guitarists Gary Rossington and Allen Collins. The group's rather cryptic name was a send-up of their high school gym teacher, Leonard Skinner, who had expelled all three of them for the length of their hair.

Nonstop touring and the combined energy of three lead guitars bolstered their first album, *Pronounced Leh-Nerd Skin-Nerd* (1973), to gold status. But it wasn't until *Second Helping* (1974), with the hit "Sweet Home Alabama," that the band took off. The song was a caustic retort to Neil Young's "Southern Man" (1970) in which Van Zant reminded Young that "a southern man don't need him around anyhow." "Free Bird" was picked up from the first album and went to Number One, and the group was well on their way to becoming successors to the Allmans' crown.

But like the Allmans, Skynyrd was struck by tragedy at the peak of their success. Two crucial members, Van Zant and guitarist/songwriter Steve Gaines, were killed in 1977 when a tour airplane crashed approaching Gillsburg, Mississippi. The surviving guitarists went on to form the Rossington-Collins Band. A decade later, they staged a Lynyrd Skynyrd reunion with Ronnie's brother Johnny Van Zant on vocals. In the manner of several other seventies' survivors, the reconditioned Skynyrd continues to run.

The American South sent groups up the national charts well into the eighties, but the spirit of southern boogie really died with the original lineups of the Allmans and Lynyrd Skynyrd. Regional scenes will always come and go, but few will ever claim rock and roll as its own as credibly as the Confederate bands of the early seventies.

Opposite, top: Kiss staged the ultimate in glitter-rock theater, spitting fire and wearing elaborate makeup that took over an hour to apply. Opposite, bottom: Vincent Furnier, a.k.a. Alice Cooper, propelled rock theater to ever more bizarre extremes while serving up classic glitter rock.

WILD HORSES:
COUNTRY ROCK

I n 1968, the Byrds' leader Roger McGuinn allowed new member Gram Parsons to persuade him to record the next Byrds album in Nashville, Tennessee, land of rhinestone cowboys and the Grand Ole Opry. The result, *Sweetheart of the Rodeo,* turned out to be a digression engineered by Parsons, a unique blend of folk, rock, and a style unfamiliar to most rock fans—country.

Although country, bluegrass, and Western swing had been crucial to the phrasing and attitude of rockabilly, the new blend borrowed from the music more directly. Parsons' country-rock fusion leaned heavily on country instrumentation and style, blending the pedal-steel guitar sweetness and romantic spirit of country music with rock's sense of urban frustration and aggressiveness. Adopted by a new generation of progressive folk rockers such as the Eagles, Firefall ("Just Remember I Love You," 1977), and Pure Prairie League ("Amie," 1975), it was a sound that would inspire musicians and record buyers alike during the mid-seventies.

Gram Parsons

Born Ingram Cecil Conner in Winter Haven, Florida, Parsons (who took his name from his mother's second husband) attended Harvard University, but left school, following the advice of then-professor and LSD guru Timothy Leary ("tune in, turn on, and drop out"). Moving to the youth mecca of Los Angeles, he made one obscure album before joining the Byrds. He left the following year in a disagreement over the group's plans to play in apartheid South Africa, and formed the Flying Burrito Brothers.

Critic Robert Christgau has hailed the first Burritos album, *Gilded Palace of Sin* (1969), as "the only full-fledged country-rock masterpiece." Apparently, the Rolling Stones agreed; they gave "Wild Horses" to Parsons for his second album, *Burrito Deluxe* (1970), and borrowed his country mannerisms for their own recording of the song in 1971. The Burritos continued to break new ground until Parsons was injured in a motorcycle accident in 1970. After a period of recovery, he recorded two solo albums that have become critics' favorites. However, before his impact could be fully absorbed, Parsons died of a drug overdose in 1973.

Buffalo Springfield and CSNY

Even without the efforts of Parsons and the Byrds, country rock was in the dry Los Angeles air during the folk-rock boom. Buffalo Springfield, which lasted only one short year between 1966 and 1967, brought a country flavor to such hits as "For What It's Worth" (about the youth riots that plagued the Sunset Strip at the time), "Bluebird," and "Rock'n'Roll Woman" (all 1967).

In Stephen Stills and Neil Young, Buffalo Springfield comprised half of the era's most brilliant aggregation of songwriting and vocal talent, Crosby, Stills, Nash & Young. David Crosby, of course, came from the Byrds, pausing along the way to produce Joni Mitchell's first album, *Songs to a Seagull* (1968), for Canada-only release. Graham Nash had been a member of a popular British Invasion group, the Hollies (named for Buddy Holly), singing lead on such hits as "Bus Stop" (1966) and "Carrie Ann" (1967).

Crosby, Stills, Nash & Young lasted only a few years before splintering into a shower of solo and duo projects (of which Young's have shown the most country influence). But in the early seventies, they added a dash of country to such hits as "Teach Your Children" (1970, featuring a rare pedal-steel performance by Grateful Dead guitarist Jerry Garcia). Perhaps more significantly, the sublime blend of their close-harmony vocal arrangements was a formative influence on pop craftsmen America ("Horse With No Name," 1973) and the Eagles.

Michael Ochs Archives

The Eagles

It was left to the Eagles, in the years following Gram Parsons' death, to become the foremost popularizers of country rock. The group was modeled after the Flying Burrito Brothers (of which drummer Bernie Leadon had been a member) and Poco (another Buffalo Springfield offshoot). Based on the vocal and songwriting talents of Don Henley and Glenn Frey, the Eagles became one of the top acts of the seventies with such country-rock smashes as "Take It Easy" (1972), "Peaceful Easy Feeling" (1972), "Best of My Love" (1974), "Lyin' Eyes" (1975), the pure-pop "One of These Nights" (1975), and the tough "Life in the Fast Lane" (1977, with James Gang guitarist Joe Walsh). The band's association with pop *chanteuse* Linda Ronstadt and singer/songwriter Jackson Browne accounts for the country influence in the early hits of those artists.

In the next decade, the country-rock torch would pass into the hands of its legitimate heirs from the country side of the fence. These include Carlene Carter (wife of British pub rocker Nick Lowe), Rosanne Cash (Johnny's daughter), Dwight Yoakum, Bonnie Raitt, Steve Earle, and Lyle Lovett, an exceptional talent who seems genuinely uncomfortable in either camp. Despite the country-rock revival of the mid-eighties that included the Beat Farmers, the Rave-Ups, the Textones, and Jason & the Scorchers, it's likely that the next generation of country-rock stars will cross over into rock from country, rather than appropriating a country vocabulary for rock and roll.

Opposite: Comprising ex-members of the Byrds, Buffalo Springfield, and the Hollies, Crosby, Stills, Nash & Young (pictured here with sidemen Greg Reeves and Dallas Taylor) injected a strong country flavor into their folk-based style. This page: The Eagles, formed in the image of Gram Parsons' Flying Burrito Brothers, made country rock a staple of the U.S. Top 40.

© Michael Putland/Retna, Ltd.

© Arthur D'Amario III/Retna, Ltd.

© Arthur D'Amario III/Retna, Ltd.

© Larry Busacca/Retna, Ltd.

BORN IN THE U.S.A.:
POST-DYLAN SINGER/ SONGWRITERS, CRAFTSMEN, AND HEROES

A s a model for mid-sixties pop stardom, Bob Dylan embodied nothing short of a paradigm shift, an entirely new kind of star. His appeal was not the dangerous macho cool of Elvis (itself simply an inversion of the clean-cut crooner), nor did he possess the cute exterior of a mop-top. And if his literary skills were unquestionable, his musical skills left much to be desired. But Dylan projected an urgency that made it clear that the voice in which he sang was entirely his own. Moreover, he truly had something to say, whether scathing political commentary or painfully private insight.

Dylan's effect on individual singer/songwriters was as dramatic as that of the Beatles on rock and roll bands. Just as the British Invaders left thousands of groups in their wake, he engendered thousands of spokespersons-for-a-generation. As Dylan's influence on musical style waned with the fading of folk rock, the more amorphous impact of his creativity manifested itself in the confessional singer/songwriter boom of the early seventies.

The Confessional Singer/Songwriters

The intimacy and immediacy of folk music was perfectly suited to the introspective mood that settled over America in the wake of Vietnam. Presenting gentle, depoliticized dispositions, singer/ songwriters such as Cat Stevens ("Wild World," 1971), Jackson Browne ("Doctor, My Eyes," 1972), Don McLean ("Vincent," 1972), and Canadian singer/novelist Leonard Cohen ("Suzanne") applied folk stylings to lyrics that bared the authors' insecurities, sensitivities, and vulnerabilities. The genre's most enduring talents are James Taylor, Carole King, and Joni Mitchell.

James Taylor, Carole King, and Carly Simon

James Taylor was picked up by the Beatles' Apple label in 1969, for which he recorded an eponymous debut album that languished in the chaos that surrounded the Fab Four at the time. In 1970, his reflection on his years of drug addiction and psychological instability, "Fire and Rain," shot to the top of the charts. It was a far cry from the social relevance of folk rock, the revolutionary stance of psychedelia, and the rebellious fun of early rock and roll. The sixties were indeed over.

The following year, Taylor recorded "You've Got a Friend" by Carole King. King had been one of the shining lights of Don Kirshner's Brill Building stable of songwriters during the early sixties, having penned such standouts as "Up on the Roof" (1962) for the Drifters and "Will You Still Love Me Tomorrow" (1960) for the Shirelles. In the wake of Taylor's success, she proved herself her own best interpreter with the release of her best-selling album *Tapestry* in 1971. Carly Simon also found a niche as a tougher sort of singer/songwriter with a caustic yet articulate anthem, "You're So Vain" (1972).

Carole King, who cut her teeth writing hits for the likes of the Monkees, came into her own as a confessional singer/songwriter.

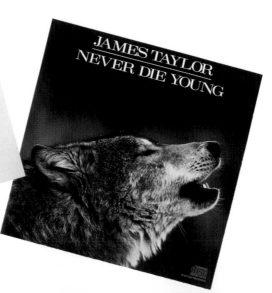

Joni Mitchell

Joni Mitchell, born in 1943 in Alberta, Canada, is one of the few from the confessional school who made a career out of putting the genre's paeans to individualism and personal growth into musical action. Possessed of a spectacularly ethereal voice and a bent for poetic abstraction, she first made an impression with folk-flavored meditations such as "Both Sides Now" (1969), "Big Yellow Taxi" (1970) and "Woodstock" (1970, made famous by Crosby, Stills, Nash & Young).

Mitchell jumped headlong into jazz-inflected pop with *Court and Spark* in 1974, a remarkably rich work that charmed the public with the hit "Help Me." After that, jazz became an increasingly prominent element in her music. During the late seventies, her band's membership was drawn from some of the best jazz-rock groups of the day, primarily Tom Scott & the L.A. Express, Weather Report, and the Pat Metheny Group.

The subtlety of Mitchell's lyrics intensified as she experimented with increasingly personal musical ideas on albums such as *Hejira* (1976). However, her audience failed to keep up with her. Her tribute to jazz innovator Charles Mingus (*Mingus,* 1979) was a commercial flop. By then the singer/songwriters had been swept away by the rising tide of punk rock.

Modern Confessions

Although the days of the confessional singer/songwriter are long gone, an artist like Mitchell can still come up with a powerful statement from time to time—as in *Night Ride Home* (1991). Paul Simon is another; his ebullient *Graceland,* introducing a number of wonderful South African musicians to a worldwide audience, was one of the highlights of 1986. Periodic folk revivals bring the confessional school back into session, revealing new talents such as Suzanne Vega ("Luka," 1987), Tracy Chapman ("Fast Car," 1988), Michelle Shocked, the Indigo Girls, and Shawn Colvin.

Pop-Rock Craftsmanship

The confessional boom also thrust into the limelight a number of talented singer/songwriters whose musical sympathies lay less with Dylan and the folk rockers than with Tin Pan Alley. Like the Brill Building stable of songwriters, including Carole King, who fueled the teen idols and girl groups of the early sixties, the Tin Pan Alley composers had domi-

Left: In 1970, James Taylor ushered in an era of quieter, more intimate, more personal rock. Above: Joni Mitchell epitomized the soul-bearing articulateness of the singer/songwriters.

© Jodi Summers Dorland/Retna, Ltd.

nated the pop music and Broadway shows two decades before. Less a movement than a by-product of the popularity of the confessionals, early-seventies pop-rock craftsmanship produced the overwrought dramatics of Neil Diamond ("I Am…I Said," 1971) and the ironic mumbling of Randy Newman ("Short People," 1977), as well as superstardom for its two most popular exponents, Elton John and Billy Joel.

Elton John

Born Reginald Kenneth Dwight in 1947, Elton John worked as an errand boy for the Beatles music publisher, Dick James, during the mid-sixties. He also played piano for the London outfit Bluesology, backing British bluesman Long John Baldry. When it came time to pick a stage name, he settled on a combination of Bluesology's sax player, Elton Dean, and Long John Baldry.

Answering an ad in a London music newspaper, he found himself teamed with lyricist Bernie Taupin in efforts to write hits for other artists. Eventually, it became clear that John should sing the songs himself. With the release of his eponymous second album in 1970, the sentimental "Your Song" became a smash hit in both Britain and North America. So began a string of albums that would be among the biggest sellers of the decade.

Meanwhile, the star cultivated a flamboyant bisexual image in keeping with the glitter-rock era. Looking like rock and roll's answer to Liberace, John staged elaborate shows that featured ever more outrageous costumes (his glasses were particularly ornate). Nonetheless, the music remained top-notch: *Madman Across the Water* (1971), *Honky Chateau* (1972), *Don't Shoot Me, I'm Only the Piano Player* (1973), and *Goodbye Yellow Brick Road* (1973) set pop-rock standards for the era. Although both his popularity and the quality of his songwriting waned during the mid-seventies and eighties, Elton John remains a chart contender in the nineties.

Elton John.

Billy Joel

Billy Joel is Elton John's American counterpart. Born in Long Island, New York in 1949, Joel performed and recorded in a number of styles before scoring his first hit in 1973 with a thoughtful ballad, "Piano Man."

But Joel proved too much a craftsman for first-person self-indulgence, and too straightforward a personality for private revelations. Instead, he concentrated on engaging stories in a traditional pop-song format, leavened by the confessional school's solipsistic air of subjectivity. His efforts finally bore fruit with the massive success of *The Stranger* in 1977, featuring "Just the Way You Are," one of the most heavily covered songs in history.

For the next three years, Joel could do no wrong, and he has been a staple of the Top Forty ever since. Fodder for supermarket tabloids ever since his marriage to supermodel Christie Brinkley, Billy Joel continues to top the charts with well-crafted songs that span the pop styles of the past four decades.

Post-Dylan American Heroes

By the mid-seventies, the music world was beginning to recognize what had been lost in the translation of rock and roll into big business. The only rational responses were either to bury one's head in the sand (disco), go with the flow (corporate rock), nuke the system (punk), or take a romantically heroic stance in the face of overwhelming commercialism.

A distinctive clique of American rockers took the latter path, mining the roots of American rock while working variations on Dylan's "spokesman-for-a-generation" pose. This American Heroic school includes Bob Seger ("Night Moves," 1976), Tom Petty & the Heartbreakers ("Refugee," 1980), John Cougar Mellencamp ("Jack and Diane," 1982), and Bruce Hornsby ("The Way It Is," 1986).

Neil Young ("Heart of Gold," 1972) is something of an anomaly in this group insofar as he has cut his own path throughout the years, speaking for no one but himself. He began as an articulate confessional singer/songwriter and has worked his way from country-flavored pop to blistering rock and roll to synthesizer gimmickry and back again, making cryptic observations on the state of America along the way. Only in hindsight is it possible to recognize him as one of the post-Dylan American Heroes, and one of rock and roll's great sages.

But the man who best embodies the American Heroic tendency is the Boss from New Jersey, the erstwhile "future of rock and roll," Bruce Springsteen.

Bruce Springsteen

Few stars can maintain a belief in rock and roll's implicit promise to change the world, and fewer still can live up to it. But Springsteen, son of a New Jersey bus driver, offers that kind of salvation to his worldwide audience. Springsteen's roots-rock approach—drawing on country, folk, and classic rock and roll—lays a rollicking foundation for lyrics that express a yearning to transcend the limitations of American bourgeois society and, at the same time, celebrate them.

Springsteen gigged tirelessly on both coasts of the United States during his teens. In 1972, Columbia Records' legendary A&R man, John Hammond, listened to him perform and heard the same quality that had prompted him to sign the young Bob Dylan. Springsteen turned out two acclaimed albums, but the audience didn't catch on until *Born to Run* in 1974. The impact on America was obvious; he occupied the covers of *Time* and *Newsweek* during 1975.

Meanwhile, concert appearances secured his reputation as one of the great rock and roll showmen. On the bleak *Nebraska* (1982), he took the unprecedented risk of releasing cassette demos rather than finished performances. The songs from that album took on an anguished political tone worthy of Dylan, a trend Springsteen continued with the smash hit *Born in the U.S.A.* (1984).

The gossip columns had a field day when he left his wife of four years, actress Julianne Phillips, in 1989, for Patti Scialfa, a member of his backup band. They later married, and now have two children.

Springsteen is rare in his insistence on maintaining an all-but-forgotten notion of integrity in rock. He routinely contributes to liberal causes, plays benefit concerts (including the 1985 "We Are the World" famine relief effort), and staunchly refuses corporate sponsorship of his tours. Every one of his post-1979 studio albums appears in *Rolling Stone*'s list of *The 100 Greatest Albums of the Eighties.* He recently released two albums in tandem in 1992. There's every indication that the future holds more Springsteen classics in store.

Bruce Springsteen.

SIMPLE DREAMS:
L.A. POP ROCK

Sunny Los Angeles has long been a land of freeways and beaches, broken dreams and Hollywood dreams-come-true. During the mid-seventies, as during the ascendency of surf rock, much of the most commercially successful music came from Los Angeles.

The City of Angels always has been, and probably always will be, a bastion of mainstream pop. As the seventies unfolded, it was the testing ground for acts like Bread ("Make It With You," 1970), Three Dog Night ("Mama Told Me Not to Come," 1970), Seals and Crofts ("Summer Breeze," 1972), and the Doobie Brothers ("Listen to the Music," 1972). As the home of the Byrds, Crosby, Stills, Nash & Young, and the Eagles, it was also the axis of country rock. Joni Mitchell sang about, and made her home in, Laurel Canyon. She drew upon L.A.'s finest to concoct the jazz-pop blend that would rocket her to stardom and profoundly influence younger singers such as Rickie Lee Jones ("Chuck E.'s in Love," 1979). Los Angeles also produced the pure pop of the Carpenters, Shaun Cassidy, and the Osmonds. Regardless of style, music from Los Angeles throughout the seventies had a quality all its own—light and upbeat, immaculate and tasteful, both as breezy as the beach and as lonely as the city itself.

Like other sounds of that decade, L.A. pop rock beat a full-scale retreat from politics and social criticism, favoring wistful songs about love lost and ebullient celebrations of love (or sex) found. Often, though, the famed California mellowness carried an undercurrent of disillusionment or cynicism—after all, Los Angeles was also the home of Frank Zappa and Captain Beefheart. It was this strain that brought out the best in Jackson Browne ("Running on Empty," 1977), Warren

Zevon ("Werewolves of London," 1978), and Little Feat ("Willin'," 1971). Linda Ronstadt, however, epitomizes Southern California during the mid-seventies more than anyone.

Linda Ronstadt

Graced with an angelic face and the voice of a songbird, Ronstadt was a fixture in the American charts between 1975 and 1980. Her influence can be heard in the voices of L.A. vocalists Karla Bonoff, Nicolette Larson, and Jennifer Warnes, as well as country stars Emmylou Harris, Carlene Carter, and Rosanne Cash.

Moving from Tucson, Arizona, to Los Angeles when she was eighteen, Ronstadt scored her first hit with a folk-rock outfit, the Stone Poneys. The song, "Different Drum" (1968), was written by the Monkees' Mike Nesmith. She made her first solo album a year later, and recruited a country-rock band that included Glenn Frey, Don Henley, Randy

© Frank S. Balthis

Meisner—three out of four of the Eagles—for her third. Success was elusive until 1975, when *Heart Like a Wheel* spawned two Number One hits, both covers of proven songs: "You're No Good" (originally recorded by Betty Everett) and "When Will I Be Loved" (originally by the Everly Brothers).

Since then, Ronstadt has proven a remarkably versatile stylist. She seems equally at home with Gilbert & Sullivan's *The Pirates of Penzance* (on Broadway in 1979), Puccini's opera *La Boheme* (New York, 1984), Mexican folk songs (*Canciones de mi Padre,* 1987), and classic ballads of the forties and fifties (three trend-setting retro albums with Nelson Riddle), not to mention covers of Roy Orbison, Buddy Holly, Neil Young, the Rolling Stones, and other greats. A craftswoman *par excellence,* Linda Ronstadt sings with a passion and commitment that transcends the slick arrangements and Top-Forty targeting of her productions.

Fleetwood Mac

The other great seventies L.A. band was Fleetwood Mac, named for drummer Mick Fleetwood and bass player John McVie. In their initial incarnation as a British blues band formed in 1967, they were relatively successful in England, but didn't dent the American charts.

The seventies, too, were difficult years for Fleetwood Mac. Internal friction resulted in the cancellation of their 1973 North American tour. Soon afterward, the group learned that their manager had sent another band out under their name. Lawsuits followed, during which most of the Macs moved to Los Angeles. Guitarist Bob Welch quit almost immediately, soon to resurface with a string of solo hits that began with "Sentimental Lady" in

Left: Linda Ronstadt's gifts as a singer and interpreter made her one of the premier exponents of the California sound during the late 1970s. Opposite: Original members of the former English blues band Fleetwood Mac. The new Fleetwood Mac burst onto the U.S. charts in 1975 with new members Lindsey Buckingham and Stevie Nicks, both of whom boasted an unfailing California pop sensibility.

1977. Visiting an L.A. studio, Mick Fleetwood met a singer/songwriter duo who had just released an excellent album called *Buckingham Nicks.* He persuaded them to join the group.

Bolstered by the songwriting, vocal, and instrumental prowess of Lindsey Buckingham and Stevie Nicks, Fleetwood Mac took off. Their first album together, *Fleetwood Mac* (1975), sent song after song to the top of the singles charts, including Nicks' trademark ballad "Rhiannon," Christine McVie's "Over My Head," and "Say That You Love Me." The next, *Rumours* (1977), was an even stronger follow-up, featuring "Second Hand News," "Go Your Own Way," "You Make Loving Fun," and the haunting "Dreams." The songs detailed interpersonal difficulties within the group—Buckingham broke up with Nicks, John McVie broke up with

Christine, and Fleetwood ended his own marriage. But Fleetwood Mac's tunefulness and light touch buoyed even the darkest moments, creating a genuine pop classic.

The California sound of Fleetwood Mac, Linda Ronstadt, the Eagles, and others was washed away by the arrival of punk and new wave, whose rough edges were more credible than L.A. pop's smooth surfaces to fans and critics alike. Individual members of those groups have managed to break through (notably the Eagles' Don Henley, whose "Boys of Summer" was one of the highlights of 1984), but times have changed. In the nineties, Los Angeles is overrun by metal bands, each with bigger hair, tighter spandex, and flashier licks than the last. It seems that the days of Southern California mellow are gone for good.

Rock and Roll Siblings

Duane and Gregg Allman (the Allman Brothers)
Robert "Kool" Bell, Ronald Bell, and Kevin Bell (Kool & the Gang)
Joe and Albert Bouchard (Blue Oyster Cult)
Johnny and Dorsey Burnette (Johnny Burnette & the Rock and Roll Trio)
Richard and Tim Butler (Psychedelic Furs)
Ali and Robin Campbell (UB40)
Karen and Richard Carpenter (the Carpenters)
Jerry and Bob Casale (Devo)
John Cipollina (Quicksilver Messenger Service) **and Mario Cipollina** (Huey Lewis & the News)
Ray and Dave Davies (the Kinks)
Don and Phil Everly (the Everly Brothers)
Neil and Tom Finn (Split Enz, Crowded House)
Tom and John Fogerty (Creedence Clearwater Revival)
Maryanne and Margie Ganser (the Shangri-Las)
Barry, Robin, and Maurice Gibb (the Bee Gees), and **Andy Gibb**
O'Kelly, Rudolph, Ronald, Ernie, and Marvin Isley (the Isley Brothers)
Jackie, Tito, Jermaine, Marlon, Michael, and Randy Jackson (the Jackson 5), and **Janet Jackson**
Gary and Martin Kemp (Spandau Ballet)
Gladys, Merald, and Brenda Knight (Gladys Knight & the Pips)
Paul McCartney (the Beatles) **and Mike McGear** (Scaffold)
Mark and Bob Mothersbaugh (Devo)
Art and Cyril Neville (the Meters, the Neville Brothers)
Alan, Wayne, Merrill, Jay, Donny, and Jimmy Osmond (the Osmonds), and **Marie Osmond**
Chuck and John Panozzo (Styx)
Debbi and Vicki Peterson (the Bangles)
Ruth, Anita, and Bonnie Pointer (the Pointer Sisters)
Jeff, Steve, and Mike Porcaro (Toto)
Tommy and Bob Stinson (the Replacements)
Sylvester and Freddie Stewart (Sly & the Family Stone)
Ralph Vierra, Arthur, Antone, Feliciano, and Perry Lee Tavares (Tavares)
James, Livingston, Alex, and Kate Taylor (all solo artists)
Eddie and Alex Van Halen (Van Halen)
Ronnie Van Zant (Lynyrd Skynyrd), **Donnie Van Zant** (.38 Special), and **Johnny Van Zant** (solo artist)
Jimmy Vaughan (the Fabulous Thunderbirds) **and Stevie Ray Vaughan**
Harold and Stanley Wade (the Trammps)
Betty and Mary Weiss (the Shangri-La's)
Brian, Dennis, and Carl Wilson (the Beach Boys)
Ann and Nancy Wilson (Heart)
Cindy and Ricky Wilson (the B-52's)
Johnny and Edgar Winter (solo artist, The Edgar Winter Group)
Malcolm and Angus Young (AC/DC), **and George Young** (the Easybeats)

EASY SKANKIN':

REGGAE AND OTHER INTERNATIONAL VARIATIONS

The appeal of rock and roll is international, and so is its influence. Upon contact with Western pop music, folk traditions across the globe have blossomed into a plethora of exotic hybrids. In Brazil, it's the tropicalismo of Milton Nascimento. In Trinidad, it's soul-calypso, or soca, as set forth by Mighty Sparrow and Lord Nelson. Puerto Rico's salsa is increasingly popular in the major cities of the United States, as are the merengue of the Dominican Republic and the compas of Haiti. The fertile soil of Africa has nurtured highlife (Ghana), juju (Nigeria), mbaqanga (Zimbabwe), rai (Algeria), and dozens of other local styles. And from the Middle East, there's Ofra Haza's Yemenite dance pop.

Of course, such influences are a two-way street. In a curious cultural feedback loop, third-world hybrids boomerang back to North America and Britain, influencing rock on its own turf. As early as 1961, the Tokens appropriated an irresistible African folk melody for their doo-wop classic "The Lion Sleeps Tonight." During the late seventies and early eighties, the Police adopted the rhythms and arrangements, even the *patois* of Jamaican reggae, and Paul Simon limned his 1986 masterpiece *Graceland* with sprightly African rhythms and guitar figures.

Reggae is the most well known of rock and roll's international variations. Its relationship to Western pop music serves as representative of other third-world hybrids.

Opposite: The late Bob Marley was reggae's greatest exponent. He was poised on the brink of international superstardom at the time of his death in 1981.

When Jamaica's first radio station began transmitting in 1959, Jamaicans began buying radios. Before long, they were grooving to the R&B, gospel, and nascent rock and roll broadcast by stations in Miami and New Orleans.

Given the island's hobbled economy, performing bands were scarce, and DJs became indispensable for dances and parties. They traveled with large public address systems that came to be known as "sound systems." American records were all over the airwaves, but they weren't available in Jamaican stores. Since the DJ with the best records stood to reap the biggest financial rewards, intense rivalries developed. Violent incidents were frequent as records were stolen and recovered. The sound-system scene took on an atmosphere of gangsterism, and record collections were commonly supervised by armed guards.

The solution was to record covers of American hits in Jamaica and press only enough copies for use by an individual sound system. When native musicians raised on Jamaican folk music—a style called mento that dates back to the turn of the century—tried to play R&B, they inevitably gave it a distinctive spin. By 1962, the fusion was called ska.

Ska was played at a frantic pace, emphasizing the polkalike accents of mento, which fell on the music's upbeats. Ska had a heyday in Britain during the early sixties—the Beatles' "Ob-La-Di, Ob-La-Da" (1968) was an overt attempt to emulate the style—and again twenty years later when groups such as the Specials, Madness, UB40, and the English Beat initiated a ska revival (called "two-tone" because it welcomed both black and white musicians). Over time, the tempo began to slow down, and ska became rock steady. Americans got a taste of the new style when a song by Desmond Dekker & the Aces, "The Israelites," became a novelty hit during the late sixties.

The title of "The Israelites" reflects the religious flavor that devotees of the Rastafarian sect were beginning to inject into Jamaican pop. Emerging during the 1930s, Rastafarianism combined pan-African nationalism with elements of Christianity and African folk religions. The Rastas' emphasis on African culture brought with it an infusion of African rhythmic finesse that had been lacking from mento, ska, and rock steady. Laying a polyrhythmic

lattice over a still slower version of rock steady, the Rastafarian musicians invented reggae.

The style's name has been related to the words "ragged" or everyday, and "regular" as in a steady beat. The late, great Bob Marley, however, insisted that "reggae" means "the king's music," a reference to Ethiopian King Haile Selassie, whom the Rastas regard as an incarnation of the Godhead. In any case, the word first appeared in 1968 with Toots & the Maytals' "Do the Reggay."

The new sound reached North America a short time later with the release of the film *The Harder They Come* (1971) starring Jimmy Cliff. This true story of a reggae singer-turned-gangster gained a cult following in America partly due to an excellent soundtrack made up of early reggae hits. Paul Simon appropriated a ska-influenced sound for "Mother and Child Reunion" in 1972, announcing it as reggae, and Eric Clapton parlayed it into a hit two years later with his cover of Bob Marley & the Wailers' "I Shot the Sheriff." Led Zeppelin even jumped on the reggae bandwagon with "D'Yer Mak'er" (1973), the title of which, pronounced with the appropriate brogue, is a pun on "Jamaica."

Bob Marley is reggae's shining star and its fallen hero. Between his first recording in 1964 and his death from cancer in 1981 at age thirty-five, he rose to international stardom on the strength of his musical mastery, moral authority, and unerring hipness. Had he lived, undoubtedly he would have become one of the world's most popular black stars. Instead, he left behind a collection of recordings that are among the best that reggae has to offer, including the classics "Is This Love" (1978, covered by Carly Simon in 1983) and "No Woman No Cry" (1981).

Reggae, along with its dub and toasting variations, continues to be the dominant music in Jamaica, and remains popular in North America and Britain. With Marley's death, however, it's unlikely that reggae will become a major force in rock and roll—at least, not until another artist of his stature comes along, which isn't likely to happen soon.

THE SOUND OF PHILADELPHIA:
PHILLY SOUL

With the beginning of the singer/songwriter boom in 1970, African-American music lost much of its power over the white mainstream. The prime movers of Motown and the nascent funk sound continued to turn out masterpieces, but these were isolated efforts rather than vectors of an identifiable movement. In the short time that remained before disco's sneak attack on the American psyche, a posse of black producers from Philadelphia filled the vacuum with the sleek, sophisticated sound of Philly soul.

During the halcyon days of the teen idols, Philadelphia's hit factories had churned out lily-white fantasies for affluent suburban teens. But behind the scenes, many of the faces were black. In 1958, producer and songwriter Kenny Gamble helped fashion "At the Hop" — sort of a bleached "Twist and Shout" — for Danny & the Juniors. Meanwhile, Leon Huff played backing tracks on a number of white-bread records. As Gamble & Huff, they began producing soul novelties during the late sixties with only regional success. Their long-standing working relationship both with one another and with the rest of the Philly scene played no small part in the relaxed groove that propelled later hits on their own Philadelphia International label.

Gamble & Huff's first national break came with a string of 1969 hits for Jerry Butler, formerly of the Impressions, beginning with "Only the Strong Survive." Influenced by Dionne Warwick's late-sixties hits as well as the successes of fellow Impression Curtis Mayfield (whose *Superfly* soundtrack was one of the soul highlights of 1971), they began working on a formula for mainstream crossover.

By 1972, they were hitting pay dirt with Billy Paul ("Me and Mrs. Jones"), Harold Melvin & the Blue Notes ("If You Don't Know Me by Now"), and most spectacularly with the O'Jays ("Back Stabbers"). The style was Motown-derived in its loping rhythms, but sweetened by unison strings and decidedly less raucous. Leaning heavily on unusual instruments such as vibraphone and harpsichord, Philly soul was cool, sophisticated, and sexy.

During the following year, Gamble & Huff laid the foundation for the anonymous four-on-the-floor pulse of disco, but their stable nonetheless turned out a body of distinctive work, including "Love Train" by the O'Jays. In fact, "TSOP (the Sound of Philadelphia)" by the label's house band MFSB, was one of the top-selling singles of 1974. That year also delivered the Stylistics syrupy ballad "You Make Me Feel Brand New" and the O'Jays' timeless funk potboiler, "For the Love of Money."

By the end of 1974, Gamble & Huff productions accounted for ten national hit singles. Their stiffest local competition, producer Thom Bell (of the Delfonics "Ready or Not, Here I Come" and the Spinners' "I'll Be Around"), racked up eleven. The Philadelphia sound was so ubiquitous that David Bowie, in search of the ingredient that gave the best African-American music its undeniable authority, went to Philadelphia International's annex, Sigma Sound, to record *Young Americans* in 1975.

The incipient disco craze was the perfect outlet for Philly soul's honey-sweet arrangements, cool grooves, and restrained sexuality. With the Trammps' "Disco Inferno," the highlight of the soundtrack to the disco epic *Saturday Night Fever,* Philly soul turned the corner. Although the Philadelphia scene continued to fuel the Top Forty throughout the seventies, disco and its evil twin, funk, took over as the primary vehicles for black rock until the end of the decade.

Left: Kenny Gamble and Leon Huff, the production team responsible for the sleek sound of Philadelphia soul during the early 1970s. Opposite: Disco diva Donna Summer mesmerized dancers with her ecstatic moans in "Love to Love You, Baby."

Michael Ochs Archives

SHAKE YOUR BOOTIE:
Disco

Much reviled and, in the nineties, nearly forgotten, the disco era was one of the biggest and most baffling phenomena ever to ruffle the calm exteriors of the power brokers who run the music industry. Springing first from the discotheques of New York, then those of Philadelphia and Miami—dance clubs patronized almost exclusively by gay men—disco offered a liberating vision of hip-grinding ecstasy to a world overwhelmed by the unfulfilled idealism of the sixties and numbed by the crass commercialism of the seventies' corporate rock. Disco was an escape into the sensory overload of a floor full of writhing bodies bathed in the kaleidoscopic vortex of a mirror ball. It was a production-line pulse on which to hang lightweight pop melodies, free of adolescent posturing and messages about social responsibility.

Negating just about every innovation of the sixties, disco discarded artistic self-expression as a goal, the album as an art form, the star as a moral authority, and the band as a model for social organization. Unlike the anything-goes boogie of rock dancing, which emphasized spontaneity and inclusiveness, disco moves were choreographed and robotic, designed to show off lithe bodies and garish clothing. But like rock and roll in its earliest days, disco was unabashedly hedonistic, a celebration of sexuality and the communality of the dance floor.

Originally, disc jockeys determined the parameters of the style. They selected from the only danceable music available in 1974: the growling love raps of Barry White, the slick urban grooves of Isaac Hayes and Curtis Mayfield, and the upwardly mobile soul stylings of the Philadelphia International stable. Dance-club exposure stimulated record sales, and the buzz that surrounds just about any underground scene brought disco to the attention of record companies, radio, and the press. By 1975, KC & the Sunshine Band were already recommending that everyone "Get Down Tonight," while Van McCoy showed them how to "Do the Hustle."

© Syndication International, Ltd.

Disco Stars: Chic, the Village People, and Donna Summer

Like most new styles, disco swept away older artists who couldn't adapt and opened the door for many others who had been knocking for years. The latter mostly included R&B, soul, and funk bands such as Chic ("Le Freak," 1978), who forged disco's only group identity. (Chic founder Nile Rodgers became one of the biggest producers of the eighties, midwifing David Bowie's *Let's Dance* and Madonna's *Like a Virgin,* among others.) But primarily disco was a producer's music. Groups were manufactured from whole cloth, such as the Village People, who reached top of the charts with a series of gay in-jokes ("In the Navy" in 1977, and "YMCA" and "Macho Man," both 1978).

Steamy diva Donna Summer became the first disco artist to escape the genre's built-in anonymity. Her "Love to Love You Baby" (1976) had listeners debating the number of orgasms represented in her vocal performance. Unlike virtually every other star of the disco era, she managed to parlay the initial attention into a career that has extended all the way into the nineties. Over the years, Summer's hits have included "I Feel Love" (1977), "Bad Girls" (1979), "On the Radio" (1980), "She Works Hard for the Money" (1981), and "This Time I Know It's for Real" (1989).

The Disco Bandwagon

Disco fashion demanded only the right tempo, a straight-ahead four-four rhythm, and a relatively sweet approach to arranging, so it didn't take much imagination to overhaul older acts. Disco rejuvenated the girl-group Patti Labelle & the Bluebelles; dressed in space-age Mardi Gras costumes as Labelle, they had a disco smash with "Lady Marmalade" (1975). Established artists jumped onto the bandwagon as well. The Bee Gees, originally second-generation British Invaders, applied their warbling falsettos to "Jive Talkin'" and "Nights on Broadway," while Elton John pounded out "Philadelphia Freedom" (all in 1975). Jazzers turned to disco as a way of creating crossover hits such as George Benson's "Breezin'" in 1976.

As a one-shot vehicle for selling singles, disco was perhaps unparalleled. The charts swarmed with get-rich-quick schemes as everything from oldies to movie themes to symphonic classics spawned disco versions. Walter Murphy presented a funked-up rendition of Beethoven's Fifth as "A Fifth of Beethoven" (1976), while former Beach Boy Bruce Johnston discoized the classic surf instrumental "Pipeline" (1977). Even the novelty "Disco Duck" (1976) by Rick Dees sold platinum.

In 1975, the twelve-inch (30-cm) single was introduced as a promotional device to encourage DJs to play new records. But soon these records were being released commercially, and the industry began an orgy of selling the same music over and over in an endless variety of "club mix" versions. In the nineties, the remix maneuver remains an effective marketing strategy, making it possible for artists from superstar Madonna to new ager Patrick O'Hearn to slap together entire new albums of old remixes. (To be fair, the disco mix is something of a formal innovation in rock and roll, deepening the notion of what, essentially, a composition is, and acknowledging for the first time in recording history the creative role of the mixdown engineer.)

John Travolta, frozen in his triumphant pose from the smash movie *Saturday Night Fever,* is an icon of the disco years.

Saturday Night Fever

As usual, mainstream recognition on a massive scale spelled the beginning of the end. In 1978, TV star John Travolta starred in the smash disco-exploitation flick *Saturday Night Fever,* which depicted a disco scene from which every evidence of homosexuality had been purged and the best dancers were white Brooklynites. The soundtrack album yielded three hits for the Bee Gees, "Night Fever," "How Deep is Your Love," and "More Than a Woman," and one for the Trammps, an eleven-minute dance-floor epic, the towering "Disco Inferno." The two-record set held the title of best-selling pop album of all time until Michael Jackson's *Thriller* overtook it in 1981.

Concurrently, post–British Invasion stalwart Rod Stewart went disco with "Do Ya Think I'm Sexy." Even the Rolling Stones finally bit the bullet, landing their biggest hit in years, "Miss You." Blondie countered from the new wave camp in 1979 with "Heart of Glass," while AOR prima donnas Queen appropriated the bass line for "Another One Bites the Dust" from Chic's "Good Times."

Disco Sucks

But while these songs were among the biggest sellers of the late seventies, the rock audience never quite went for it. Disco was too closely associated with black artists, and perhaps too close to gay culture, to be embraced by the white mainstream. Besides, much of the music the genre produced—save the best of it, which qualified equally as soul or light funk—inspired legitimate complaints of inanity, superficiality, and anonymity. Anti-disco sentiment mounted as rock fans rallied around the slogan "disco sucks!"

For all its longevity, disco was, in the end, merely a "trend," never really establishing itself as an independent style. Unlike punk, rap, or other enduring styles dismissed as fads in their day, it failed to generate its own core of stars capable of moving records in the huge numbers to which the majors had become accustomed. With eyes trained squarely on the bottom line, the industry pulled the plug on the promotion machine, and disco sank like a stone.

Disco Lives

Actually, disco never really died; it simply muddled through without the unifying forces of a name and a subculture. From the ashes of disco rose ex-model Grace Jones ("Pull Up to the Bumper Baby," 1981) and the newly reconditioned Michael Jackson, whose "Don't Stop 'Til You Get Enough," (1977) propelled him to unparalleled heights of megastardom during the eighties. A short time later, Madonna would emerge from the sweaty dance clubs of New York City. Outside of the glare of the Top Forty, the disco era spawned punk-dance bands like New Order, as well as some of the major movements of the nineties, including the current Chicago house craze and the Manchester scene in England (the Soup Dragons, EMF, Happy Mondays).

Despite the derision of rock fans, disco reminded everyone that dancing is an indispensable accoutrement to pop music. The relentless hi-hat and bass drum of disco marks the beginning of a revitalization of the groove that invigorated the eighties (Bowie's "Let's Dance," Peter Gabriel's "Sledgehammer") and infuses nearly every branch of rock and roll in the nineties. Not bad, for music that sucked.

Ex-model Grace Jones appropriated the decadence of disco culture to produce haunting dance rock.

ONE NATION UNDER A GROOVE:
FUNK

In a sense, disco spelled the end of soul as the grass-roots music of black America. The successes of Motown and rock'n'soul had reoriented African-American musicians toward the white market. Now, the dance imperative diverted the attention of virtually every soul talent toward the crossover carrot that dangled enticingly overhead.

But, along with disco, another strain of mutant soul had evolved, represented in the charts by Rufus ("Tell Me Something Good," 1974, featuring Chaka Khan), the Ohio Players ("Fire," 1974), Kool & the Gang ("Hollywood Swingin'," 1974), the Average White Band ("Pick Up the Pieces," 1974), and erstwhile balladeers the Commodores ("Brickhouse," 1977, featuring Lionel Richie). An elaboration of Memphis soul's sledgehammer groove, this style had been developing in relative isolation for nearly a decade. Named for an obscure term denoting a pungent odor—like "rock and roll," a phrase that probably originated in the brothels of urban black ghettos—it was known as funk. By the time disco had chiseled out a niche for dance music in the mid-seventies, funk responded with a sound that was harder, sweatier, and nastier than disco.

Funk is disco's reckless older brother. Its beats tend to be more syncopated, its arrangements less formulaic, its tempos more varied, its emphasis less on songs than on grooves. By and large, funk depends on the interaction of a band, rather than a producer and a multitrack tape recorder, in order to build up a serious head of steam. Funk bands were bent on reclaiming the gritty, real-life quality of the blues and gospel for rock and roll, while at the same time flaunting their African heritage.

As a stylistic tag for African-American music, funk first turned up in the title of Dyke & the Blazers' "Funky Broadway" (1967). Even by then, however, the musical underpinnings of the style were well established. They had been pioneered, more or less single-handedly, by James Brown.

James Brown

From the vantage point of the early nineties, James Brown is the towering figure of African-American popular music. In a career that spans well over three decades, he helped to distinguish soul from gospel and R&B, pioneered funk, and forged the raw materials of rap. He also gained a reputation as one of the most dynamic live performers ever. And throughout the tumult of the sixties, Brown projected an image of black power that, in its focus on education and self-reliance, continues to exercise a positive influence.

Brown's is a classic rags-to-riches story. Born in 1928 and raised in Augusta, Georgia, he grew up shining shoes on the steps of WDRW radio, a station he would later purchase. By 1956, he had worked as a professional boxer, played drums and keyboards in a number of small-time gospel bands, and landed in reform school for car theft and breaking and entering. That year, he released his first gospel-blues single with the Famous Flames, "Please, Please, Please." Although hampered by King Records' limited distribution, the song managed to have enough of an impact to end up in a cover version on the Who's first album.

Brown continued to release raw soul records into the sixties. But with its initial sour blast of brass, "Papa's Got a Brand New Bag" (1965) shattered the soul formula, fragmenting the instrumental arrangement into a weave of intertwined but discontinuous parts. The bass line gouged out the groove, while the brass stabbed in staccato bursts. And when the band broke for the hook, the guitar's backbeat strokes skidded unaccompanied into a dissonant machine-gun solo, with that deafening horn blast hot on its heels.

From there, Brown seemed to coast into groove heaven with a series of classic singles: "I Got You (I Feel Good)" (1965), "Cold Sweat" (1967), "I Got the Feelin'" (1968), "Mother Popcorn" (1969), "Super Bad" (1970), and "Get on the Good Foot" (1972), to hit only the highest points. (His tally of over forty Top-Forty hits in the United States is surpassed only by the Beatles and Elvis Presley.) Brown goosed his players with inhuman squeals, grunts, and hollers, directing the form of each song on the fly with last-minute instructions such as "To the bridge!" It was, indeed, a brand new bag.

Brown continued to record throughout the eighties, scoring a hit with "Living in America" (1986), from the soundtrack for *Rocky IV.* Regrettably, megalomania and drug abuse caught up with him in 1988, when he was involved in a high-speed car chase across state lines. The incident landed him in prison for two concurrent six-year sentences, from which he was only recently paroled.

Despite the brilliance of his records and stage shows, Brown's music has had limited appeal outside the African-American community. Sly Stone, however, helped to widen the reach of funk.

Opposite: James Brown, the "Godfather of Soul" and a dynamic performer onstage, helped to differentiate soul from gospel and R&B, and forged the raw materials of rap.

Sly & the Family Stone

Formed in 1966, Sly & the Family Stone was the great integrated band of the decade. The group comprised whites and blacks, men and women, attired in outrageous costumes that combined Vegas chintz with psychedelic visions. Their music started with rock'n'soul's characteristic stomp, then embellished it with snazzy horn lines, raucous chants, and an attack dose of hard-rock guitar.

Where James Brown aimed his messages at the heart of the black community, Sly Stone—like Hendrix—was a hippie at heart. (He produced Grace Slick & the Great Society's original version of "Somebody to Love.") Preaching interracial brotherhood united by the almighty groove, the group made an impression among denizens of the psychedelic underground. A string of definitive funk hits followed, including "Dance to the Music" (1967), "Everyday People" (1968), "Stand" (1969), "Thank You Falettinme Be Mice Elf Agin" (1970), and "Family Affair" (1971).

But success had a destabilizing effect on Sly, and he sank into drug dependency and erratic behavior characterized by frequent no-shows at concerts. (In 1970, the band cancelled twenty-six out of seventy bookings.) Financial difficulties, mediocre records, and a failed publicity stunt—Sly's marriage onstage at Madison Square Garden in 1974— only fueled his demise. During their moment in the limelight, however, Sly & the Family Stone showed that funk was capable of bringing together both black and white under one musical banner.

George Clinton's Parliament/ Funkadelic

If anyone is responsible for defining funk as something more than music—a style of dress, an attitude, a philosophy, a way of life—it's George Clinton. Clinton is the Frank Zappa of black rock, a prolific *auteur* who posits funk as the answer for the existential dilemmas of humanity—or at least for whatever blandness currently monopolizes the charts.

In 1968 Clinton transformed his Temptations-style group, the Parliaments, into Funkadelic, a funk band incorporating the hard grooves of Sly, the open-endedness of Hendrix, the mythic richness of avant-jazzer Sun Ra, and enough catchy sloganeering to fuel an ad agency ("Think! It ain't illegal yet"). Funkadelic mutated into a plethora of vehicles through which Clinton spread the word, including Parliament, Bootsy's Rubber Band, Parlette, the P-Funk All Stars, and the Brides of Funkenstein.

Funkadelic finally made a dent in the national consciousness in 1978 with the butt-shaking *One Nation Under a Groove.* Since then, Clinton has become ubiquitous, scoring a dance-club smash with "Atomic Dog" in 1983 and producing records for numerous Funkadelic spin-offs. By 1987, Clinton's productions numbered fifty-six.

Earth, Wind & Fire

While Clinton positioned funk in opposition to the mainstream, Earth, Wind & Fire used it to effect a full-scale takeover during the late seventies. Veteran session drummer Maurice White formed the group in 1970. Inspired by the jazz saxophonist

Opposite: George Clinton. Center: Sly Stone.

Rock and Roll Hall of Fame Inductees

1986
Chuck Berry
James Brown
Ray Charles
Sam Cooke
Fats Domino
The Everly Brothers
Buddy Holly
Jerry Lee Lewis
Elvis Presley
Little Richard

1987
The Coasters
Eddie Cochran
Bo Diddley
Aretha Franklin
Marvin Gaye
Bill Haley
B.B. King
Clyde McPhatter
Ricky Nelson
Roy Orbison
Carl Perkins
Smokey Robinson
Big Joe Turner
Muddy Waters
Jackie Wilson

1988
The Beach Boys
The Beatles
The Drifters
Bob Dylan
The Supremes

1989
Dion (Dion & the Belmonts)
Otis Redding
The Rolling Stones
The Temptations
Stevie Wonder

1990
Hank Ballard (the Midnighters)
Bobby Darin
The Four Seasons
The Four Tops
The Kinks
The Platters
Simon & Garfunkel
The Who

1991
LaVern Baker
The Byrds
John Lee Hooker
The Impressions
Wilson Pickett
Jimmy Reed
Ike & Tina Turner

1992
Bobby "Blue" Bland
Booker T and the MGs
Johnny Cash
The Jimi Hendrix Experience
The Isley Brothers
Sam & Dave
The Yardbirds

John Coltrane's integration of spirituality and music, he conceived an ensemble that would inject popular music with positive spiritual values.

EW&F finally hit in 1975. That year's *That's the Way of the World,* featuring the smash hit "Shining Star," shimmered with rhythmic subtlety, infectious grooves, and a relentlessly positive outlook. The nine-piece group drew heavily on both James Brown and Sly, but their funk was elegant, with a smooth wash of jazz. In performance, they combined stunning theatricality with equally stunning displays of instrumental virtuosity.

Subsequent releases found the group espousing a funk mysticism not unlike that of Sly and George Clinton, propped up by fanciful album-cover imagery of Egyptian motifs. "Sing a Song" broke in 1975, followed by "Getaway" (1976), "Serpentine Fire" (1977), and the ballad "After the Love Is Gone" (1979). In establishing sophistifunk as a viable approach to the Top Forty, Earth, Wind & Fire set the stage for the return of Michael Jackson.

Michael Jackson

The youngest member of the Motown stable, Michael Jackson had won over the pop audience by the time he was ten years old. Boasting moves that rivalled James Brown's and an air of maturity befitting an entertainer twice his age, he put heart and soul into his great early hits with the Jackson Five: "I Want You Back" (1970), "ABC" (1970), "I'll Be There" (1970), and "Never Can Say Goodbye" (1971).

Side by side with the group, Jackson was a solo success throughout the seventies. Beginning in 1979, though, Jackson began redefining the scope of pop stardom. Under the direction of master producer Quincy Jones, he stripped the EW&F formula down to its lowest common denominator, without sacrificing musical richness or excitement. The result was commercial dynamite.

Powered by the kinetic post-disco of "Don't Stop 'Til You Get Enough," their first effort, *Off the Wall,* became the best-selling album ever by an African-American artist. The follow-up, *Thriller* (1982), was even more devastating. Virtually every cut reached the Top Ten, most notably "Billie Jean" and "Beat It" (featuring a guitar solo by Eddie Van Halen). *Thriller* sold an astonishing 35 million copies, displacing *Saturday Night Fever* as the best-selling album of all time. Michael Jackson was suddenly the hottest property in show business.

The next album, *Bad,* a full five years in coming, was well below par musically. Still, it fueled Michaelmania, which ballooned despite reports of the star's eccentricities. Jackson's face, increasingly distorted by cosmetic surgery, expressed an innocence that made it easy to sympathize with stories that he owned a roomful of mannequins that he considered his closest friends.

Even as his meticulous pop funk captured an awesome share of the mass market, Jackson's nemesis, Prince Rogers Nelson (a.k.a. Prince), was moving an impressive number of records—and moving funk forward.

Opposite: In the years before Michael Jackson emerged as a major star and cultural icon, he and his brothers created some of Motown's greatest moments.

Prince

The young lion of black rock, Prince, was born in Minneapolis in 1959. Although he isn't an innovator on the order of his predecessors, he does embody something of James Brown's rhythmic brilliance, Sly's synthesis of black and white, and Hendrix's exotic mystery—and he's a more adventurous songwriter than any of them. Prince also adds an obsession with sexuality that has sent skyrocketing the blood pressure of defenders of American culture such as the Parents Music Resource Center. Controversy surrounding the explicit nature of his lyrics tends to obscure Prince's brilliance as a songwriter and instrumentalist, and his role in gaining recognition for talents such as Sheila E., Morris Day, Sheena Easton (for whom he wrote "Sugar Walls" in 1986), and producers Jimmy Jam and Terry Lewis.

Early in his career, Prince was looking for inspiration to fuel his songwriting. When his manager suggested that he write about sex, Prince took it to heart. By his third album in 1981, *Dirty Mind,* he was taking on subjects such as oral sex and incest without a flinch. His early records attracted little attention, but in 1984, *Purple Rain,* accompanied by the film of the same name (which he wrote, directed, and starred in), catapulted him to international stardom, where he has remained ever since.

As the eighties came to a close, Prince straddled the fence between mass acceptance and street credibility. He contributed to the soundtrack of the blockbuster movie *Batman,* then created a stir in the dance music underground by withdrawing from release a raunchy party record called *The Black Album* at the last minute. (Bootleg copies became prized commodities on the black market.) Given his age and enormous talent, it's a safe bet that Prince has more controversies in store.

Opposite: Denizens of the early-1980s Minneapolis scene led by Prince: producers Terry Lewis and Jimmy Jam (top), Sheila E. (right), and Morris Day (bottom). This page: Rick James.

Funk of the Eighties and Nineties

During the eighties, the commercial edge of the funk scene was represented by Rick James ("Super Freak," 1981, recently the basis for Hammer's "U Can't Touch This"), Chaka Khan ("I Feel for You," 1984, written by Prince), and Michael's little sister Janet Jackson ("What Have You Done for Me Lately," 1986).

The early nineties have seen a resurgence of funk in a number of unlikely places: the psychedelic dance-rock coming out of Britain, the neodisco beat of Chicago house music, and the funk-metal movement churning on America's West Coast. But funk has become eclipsed by the overwhelming popularity of rap, which has incorporated and overtaken it. Rap is now the standard-bearer of the African-American community, and the cutting edge of rock. Funk is dead. Long live funk.

JAZZ INFLUENCES

Rock and roll history has been characterized by fusions with other styles, from country to blues to folk to innumerable third-world traditions. By the early seventies, jazz fusions played a major role as well, and jazz maintains a prominent spot in the rock and roll landscape of the nineties.

The connection between rock and jazz is a family relationship. During the forties and fifties, jazz bands occasionally spiced up their repertoires with early R&B, and R&B ensembles warmed up with jazz improvisations. Jazz even seeped into the country side of rock and roll via Western swing bands like Bob Wills and his Texas Playboys (and thus into bluegrass).

Miles Davis and Jazz-Rock Fusion

Jazz enigma Miles Davis—the David Bowie of jazz, if you will—first made the connection explicit in 1969 with *Bitches Brew,* one of the great watersheds of the era. *Bitches Brew* propelled the jazz band with rock and roll rhythms, and electrified it with rock and roll instrumentation, including wah-wahs and fuzz boxes for Davis' trumpet. The great pioneers of jazz-rock fusion, virtually all of whom played on the album, have been working out the implications ever since: Chick Corea with Return to Forever and the Electrik Band, John McLaughlin with his Mahavishnu Orchestra, Herbie Hancock with Headhunters and the Rockit Band, Josef Zawinul and Wayne Shorter with Weather Report, Tony Williams with Lifetime.

Santana

The first rock band to pick up on *Bitches Brew* was Santana, led by young guitarist Carlos Santana. The Santana Blues Band came together in San Francisco's Latino district, the Mission, in 1966, on the eve of the city's psychedelic era. Playing a unique blend of fiery blues rock with Latino and African cross-rhythms, the group placed four singles in the Top Twenty in 1970, including "Evil Ways" and "Black Magic Woman."

Carlos Santana soon became involved with spiritual master Sri Chinmoy, among whose disciples was *Bitches Brew* guitarist John McLaughlin. McLaughlin encouraged Santana to submit his eloquent phrasing and fluid sense of melody to the discipline of jazz, setting the rock and roller off on a course that would keep his band away from the charts for several years. Their audience, however, continued to grow, and with it the audience for jazz-rock fusion. Today, Santana is one of the nation's most highly respected guitarists and rock's most successful Latino star.

Musicians with stronger roots in R&B and pop were beginning to explore the jazz connection as well. Blues-rock bands such as Blood, Sweat & Tears ("Spinning Wheel," 1969), Electric Flag, and Chase added a brass section, borrowing from big bands like Maynard Ferguson's and Stan Kenton's. One such group, Chicago, went on to become one of the most successful American groups in history.

Chicago

Chicago began in 1968 as Chicago Transit Authority, shortening their name when the city's Mayor Daly threatened to sue. Their early records featured extended big-bandish workouts that wed volatile brass arrangements, a hard-rocking rhythm section, and a surprisingly progressive sensibility (not to mention embarrassing liner notes in support of "the revolution in all its forms").

But in 1971, "Color My World," a sensitive ballad by pianist Robert Lamm, sowed the seeds of a change. During the coming years, Chicago tapered off its progressive approach, concentrating on the syrupy radio hits that came to characterize their career, including "(I've Been) Searchin' So Long" (1974), "If You Leave Me Now" (1976), "Hard for Me to Say I'm Sorry" (1982), the exceptionally energetic "Hard Habit to Break" (1984), "Look Away" (1988), and "You're Not Alone" (1989). The group appears likely to continue jamming the airwaves well into the nineties.

Opposite: The late trumpeter Miles Davis (left) electrified jazz and blended it with rhythms derived from rock and roll, forever changing the face of both jazz and rock. Above: Carlos Santana and his band spiced their hard-edged rock with Latin rhythms and jazz virtuosity.

Steely Dan

The sardonic Steely Dan, named for the steam-powered metal dildo in William S. Burroughs' novel *Naked Lunch,* took a nearly opposite approach. The group, actually a constellation of musicians revolving around Walter Becker and Donald Fagan, began with poppish rock tunes, gradually fortifying their arrangements with jazz harmonies and instrumentation to create one of the most satisfying jazz-rock blends. "Do It Again" and "Reelin' in the Years" kicked off their career in 1973.

Katy Lied (1975) deepened the group's reliance on jazz session players, and by *Aja* (1977) Becker and Fagan were employing the best jazz-rockers in L.A., including Steve Gadd, Lee Ritenour, Tom Scott, Larry Carlton, Steve Khan, and Weather Report's Wayne Shorter. "Hey Nineteen," in 1980, was their last hit before an acrimonious breakup. Becker and Fagan periodically announce plans to reform Steely Dan, though a reunion has yet to take place.

In hiring jazz musicians to play pop rock, Steely Dan (along with singer/songwriter Joni Mitchell) set the tone for much of the jazz-influenced pop of the eighties. When ex-Police singer Sting tired of his superstar position, he headed in the same direction.

Sting

Before the Police hit it big with their reggae-tinged rock, former schoolteacher Gordon Sumner (a.k.a. Sting) had been a denizen of London's jazz scene. In fact, it was his frustration with the realities of playing jazz for a living that originally led him into the Police. Once his commercial viability was established, he returned to his first love.

In early 1985, Sting called a jam session of major New York jazz talent. From those who showed up, he selected four of the top players in the field, including sax player Branford Marsalis, keyboardist Kenny Kirkland, and drummer Omar Hakim. Their first record, *Dream of the Blue Turtles* (1985), set a cool, sophisticated groove beneath Sting's increasingly introspective lyrics. The album immediately sold platinum, yielding the hit "If You Love Somebody, Set Them Free" and confirming Sting as one of the most popular artists of the eighties. Meanwhile, he continued the acting career that began with the 1980 adaptation of the Who's rock opera, *Quadrophenia,* appearing in *The Bride* and *Plenty* in 1985.

Continuing in the same jazz-infused vein, Sting garnered further hits and acclaim with the albums *...Nothing Like the Sun* (1987) and *The Soul Cages* (1991). He is also a staple performer at benefit concerts for Amnesty International, the Prince's Trust, and other charities.

Anita Baker

In many ways, jazz is more closely allied to soul than to the branches of the rock family tree dominated by white musicians. Anita Baker uses lush jazz settings to impart an aura of seductive passion, as well as sharp intelligence, to her pop-soul stylings. Her second album, *Rapture* (1986), was a surprise hit, establishing her immediately as one of the decade's most spectacular vocalists. Baker has continued to aim her music straight at the heart with the Grammy-winning *Giving You the Best That I Got* (1988) and *Compositions* (1990), both of which have lifted her into the highest tier of pop artists performing for an adult audience.

In the pop mainstream, Anita Baker's success was foreshadowed by the jazzy stylings of Nigerian vocalist Sade ("Smooth Operator," 1985). On the other side of the tracks, the New York avant garde has been incorporating jazz into anarchic performances by the likes of the Lounge Lizards and John Zorn. It seems to be one of the characteristics of the nineties that an artist's stylistic definitions can dissolve and reconstitute with amazing ease, and that the market can follow every permutation without losing interest. Jazz offers a powerful expressive option that more and more rock musicians see fit to exercise.

What They Were Called Before You Heard of Them

Al & the Silvertones	The Guess Who
Alan Price Combo	The Animals
American Express	Huey Lewis & the News
Angel & the Snake	Blondie
The Bank Street Blues Band	Southside Johnny & the Asbury Jukes
The Beefeaters, The Jet Set	The Byrds
The Big Thing	Chicago
The Brothers Gibb	The Bee Gees
The Canadian Squires, Levon & the Hawks	The Band
The Crossfires	The Turtles
The Deltas	The Hollies
Carl & the Passions	The Beach Boys
The Committee	The Communards
Country Zeke & the Freaks	Little Feat
Earth	Black Sabbath
The Falling Spikes	The Velvet Underground
Farmer John's Backyard Crows	The Black Crowes
The Farriss Brothers	INXS
The Four Aims	The Four Tops
Free At Last	Free
The Golliwogs, The Blue Velvets	Creedence Clearwater Revival
The Heartbeats	Herman's Hermits
Hotlegs	10cc
The Hourglass	The Allman Brothers Band
The Invaders	Madness
Johnny & the Self-Abusers	Simple Minds
The Juvenairs	Danny & the Juniors
Kippington Lodge	Brinsley Schwarz
The Lasers	Gary Numan's Tubeway Army
Mammoth	Van Halen
The Memphis Group	Booker T & the MGs
The Metropolitan Blues Quartet	The Yardbirds
The Misfits	The Go-Go's
'N Betweens, Ambrose Slade	Slade
The New Yardbirds	Led Zeppelin
The Paramounts	The Righteous Brothers
The Primettes	The Supremes
The Quarrymen, The Silver Beetles	The Beatles
The Red Roosters	Spirit
The Roundabout	Deep Purple
The Screaming Abdabs	Pink Floyd
Silence	Mott the Hoople
Silmarillion	Marillion
The Spectres, Traffic Jam	Status Quo
Stalk Forrest Group, Soft White Underbelly	Blue Oyster Cult
Sylvester Stewart	Sly Stone
Tom & Jerry	Simon & Garfunkel
The Warlocks	The Grateful Dead
Warsaw	Joy Division
Zips, London Soundtrack, Fire of London	Ultravox

WHITE LIGHT/ WHITE HEAT:

ARTY PRIMITIVISM

If anyone needed evidence in 1967 that rock and roll had turned into something other than teen entertainment, it arrived with the force of a sledgehammer in the form of *Sgt. Pepper's Lonely Hearts Club Band* by the Beatles. For the middle-class youth all over the world, the message of *Sgt. Pepper* was taken as word from on high. By joining a band, they could do something dignified. Rather than simply bashing out three-chord tunes, they could create art.

The British progressive rockers inflated three-minute pop songs into side-long epics, employing symphony orchestras and mooring their lyrics with established cultural reference points such as English literature or the great religions. In America, where cultural respectability is defined as much by sales figures as anything, a different idea bubbled to the surface. The style and form of the rock and roll song—its simplicity, directness, aggressiveness—might be suited for exploring emotional territories beyond the usual boy-meets-girl and hot-rod fantasies.

Jim Morrison's free-form rants with the Doors provided one model. Another came from an obscure group formed in New York City in 1965 in order to accommodate the songwriting eccentricities of another aspiring poet, Lou Reed. Named for a pornographic novel, Reed's band was the Velvet Underground.

The Velvet Underground

The Velvets barely made a dent in rock and roll while they were together. But in the postpunk era they are clearly one of the major influences on contemporary rock. Reed, the product of a middle-class upbringing in Brooklyn, New York, worked as a staff songwriter for Pickwick Records after graduating from college. One early Reed masterpiece, recorded by one of Pickwick's anonymous bands, instructed listeners in how to "Do the Ostrich": "You put your head on the floor and have someone step on it."

In 1965, Reed quit his job and teamed up with John Cale, a Welsh classical musician of impressive pedigree who had been seduced by New York's avant garde. Forming the Velvet Underground, they began making music that ran directly counter to the upbeat, romantic style of the day (like "I'm a Believer" by the Monkees, or the Association's "Windy"). Their songs were about heroin addiction and sadomasochism; the exhilaration and decadence of urban life. Rather than progressive, their sound was deliberately regressive, jagged and pounding, confrontational, a cacophony at the very edge of listenability.

The Velvet Underground baffled critics and audiences alike, and all four albums released during the band's lifetime, beginning with their 1967 debut with German vocalist Nico, sank into oblivion. But the songs they contained, wistful odes to redemption through exploration of the dark side of human nature, have become the stuff of legend: the tender "Pale Blue Eyes," seventeen minutes of harrowing noise called "Sister Ray," and "Sweet Jane," the closest they came to a hit. ("Sweet Jane" was covered in 1990 by the Cowboy Junkies, a Canadian band.) Although the Velvets continued in name until 1972, both Reed and Cale had left by 1970, each going on to semisuccessful solo careers and permanent cult-hero status.

Singing paeans to sadomasochism and heroin addiction, the Velvet Underground.

Michael Ochs Archives

New York Art-Punk: Patti Smith and Talking Heads

The Velvet Underground's impact on the nascent New York punk scene circa 1975 was inestimable. The New York Dolls already had updated their approach for the glitter era. Now, bands like the Ramones were revitalizing pop by stripping it down to its rawest basics, while others built on the Velvets' involvement with poetry (via Reed) and the avant garde (via Cale).

Initially inspired by the Doors, Patti Smith had been working on a blend of rock and roll and poetry since the early seventies. In 1974 she recorded a single regarded by many as the first punk record, "Piss Factory." Her reputation grew, and in 1976 she hired John Cale to produce *Horses,* a throbbing amalgam of rudimentary musicianship and Rimbaud. Smith's aggressive, literate stance made her an instant hero among intellectually minded rock fans; eventually she hit the mainstream with "Because the Night" (1978), composed in collaboration with Bruce Springsteen.

Smith's arty image was mirrored by Talking Heads, originally a trio from the Rhode Island School of Design, who rode the new wave to critical acclaim and commercial success. The Heads, though, were both less poetic and less populist than Smith. They built their music from the ground up, fleshing out leader David Byrne's quirky delivery with equally idiosyncratic arrangements that acknowledged Memphis soul even as they sounded distinctly otherworldly. Byrne observed middle-class America from a decidedly off-center perspective. His high-pitched squawk suggested that the man he sang about in "Psycho Killer" (1977) may well be himself.

By 1978, Talking Heads had perfected their sound to the extent that an ironic interpretation of Al Green's soul classic "Take Me to the River" reached Number One. Nonetheless, they remained committed to experimentation, incorporating influences from British art rock (*Fear of Music,* 1979), funk (*Speaking in Tongues,* 1983), and eventually African pop (*Naked,* 1988). The group's husband-and-wife rhythm section, Tina Weymouth

and Chris Frantz, lightened up for successes with the Tom Tom Club in 1981, while Byrne produced a film, *True Stories* (1986), and several solo albums. In the early nineties, the Heads remain the standard-bearers of rock and roll with an intellectual twist.

British Art Rock: David Bowie

The Heads' connection with British art rock began when Brian Eno produced three of their albums in the late seventies. Eno came from Roxy Music, an arty outfit led by the debonair Bryan Ferry. Ferry, in turn, had been influenced by the remarkable talents of David Bowie.

Trained in theater, mime, and graphics, Bowie is given to larger-than-life gestures that have led him to adopt a steady stream of alter egos: Ziggy Stardust, Aladdin Sane, Mr. Newton, the Thin White Duke, the Blond Fuhrer, Major Tom, and others. Although his reliance on elaborate costumes and theatrics allied him with glitter rockers in the

mold of Alice Cooper, Bowie's musical eclecticism and tireless experimentation mark him as Britain's prototypical art rocker (after, of course, the Beatles).

The Velvets' "Waiting for My Man" was part of Bowie's early concert repertoire. In fact, a 1971 meeting with Lou Reed and Andy Warhol directly inspired two songs from that year's *Hunky Dory:* "Queen Bitch," and "Andy Warhol." In 1972, the same year he made a splash with his glitter-rock classic *Ziggy Stardust & the Spiders From Mars,* Bowie produced Reed's *Transformer,* yielding the hit, "Walk on the Wild Side." As the seventies drew to a close, Bowie collaborated with Brian Eno on a trio of standout albums that flirted with avant-garde minimalism (*Low, Heroes,* and *Lodger*). By the eighties, however, he had settled on the blue-eyed soul pose that provided his greatest successes.

Opposite: David Byrne. Above: Patti Smith.

Roxy Music, Brian Eno, and Peter Gabriel

Early on, Roxy Music borrowed from Bowie a penchant for outlandish costumes and an ironic take on rock and roll. Named for the Roxy Cinema chain of movie theaters, the group evolved in the same milieu as progressives such as King Crimson and Yes. In fact, lead singer Bryan Ferry once auditioned for the lead vocal spot in Crimson; similarly, Rick Wakeman of Yes played on Bowie's *Hunky Dory.*

For their debut in 1972, Roxy Music deconstructed the late-fifties dance band and reconstituted it for the space age as a decadent, hyperromantic melange of thrashing, crooning, and distortion. Their first U.K. hit, "Virginia Plain," sounded very much like punk rock five years too early. The group underwent drastic personnel changes over the years and eventually fell by the wayside, but Ferry continues to refine his persona as a Frank Sinatra-cum-Hugh Hefner for the post-nuclear age.

Brian Eno left Roxy Music after their second album. With the group, he pioneered the use of the synthesizer as a processor of sounds coming from other members of the group. On his own, he dove into the London avant garde, coming up with a number of interesting collaborations (notably *Evening Star* with King Crimson guitarist Robert Fripp in 1974) and ground-breaking solo albums (including *Another Green World,* 1975). Main-

stream success has eluded him, but he maintains a presence as producer of such top acts as Bowie and U2 (*The Unforgettable Fire,* 1984).

A tireless moonlighter, Eno added his unique touch to a few tracks on Genesis' progressive rock masterpiece, *The Lamb Lies Down on Broadway* (1974). That was the group's last record to benefit from the talents of their mysterious front man, Peter Gabriel. Upon completion of the album, Gabriel announced to a surprised public that he had done all that he could hope to within the confines of Genesis, and promptly embarked upon a brilliant solo career exploring territory mapped out by Roxy Music, Talking Heads, and Eno.

Gabriel's first two albums failed to attract much attention, while his third and fourth made some noise with the standout cuts "Games Without Frontiers" (1980, featuring kindred spirit Kate Bush) and "Shock the Monkey" (1982). Meanwhile, Gabriel organized the World Organization of Music, Arts, and Dance (WOMAD) in order to popularize non-Western music, scored the films *Birdy* (1985) and *The Last Temptation of Christ* (1988), and experimented incessantly with high-tech musical gadgetry and third-world fusions. In 1986, the soul-flavored smash hit "Sledgehammer" confirmed Gabriel's membership in the British rock aristocracy that includes Bowie and Sting. It also provided him with the capital both to open his own recording studio and to found a record company dedicated to non-Western music called Earthworks.

Michael Ochs Archives

© Anne Fishbein/Michael Ochs Archives

Modern Art: Pere Ubu and Sonic Youth

Virtually every major figure in art rock, British and American, has graduated to fairly large scale commercial success. It's difficult to tell whether they modified their styles in pursuit of success, or whether the mainstream diverted its course to meet them. In any case, it's impossible to regard recent music by Bowie, Talking Heads, Gabriel, or Bryan Ferry as "arty primitivism." In the nineties, that title must go to bands that are, at this point, both artier and more primitive, such as Sonic Youth and Pere Ubu.

Sonic Youth is a product of the New York "noise" movement that reinterpreted punk fury in an art-rock context during the early eighties. The Youth intersperses vaguely tuneful Velvets-inspired songs with anything from chaotic feedback fests to gorgeous tone poems of backward guitars—all served up in a nonstandard tuning system that reveals the bandmembers' avant-garde roots. *Rolling Stone* magazine listed their 1988 release *Daydream Nation* among *The 100 Greatest Albums of the Eighties.*

Pere Ubu came to New York from Cleveland, Ohio, during the punk days, although they didn't make it to MTV until 1989 with *Cloudland.* Named for the classic Dadaist play by Alfred Jarry, Ubu works up a demented frenzy of industrial clatter and lurching rhythms, over which leader and vocalist David Thomas obsesses about everything from the extinction of the dinosaurs to post-war European politics. At a time when the mainstream seems capable of absorbing just about anything, the staunch individualism of bands like Ubu and Sonic Youth offers hope that the future of art rock still holds some surprises.

Opposite: Roxy Music, fronted by Bryan Ferry, reconstituted the late-1950s dance band for the space age as a decadent melange of thrashing, crooning, and distortion. Above: Having pioneered rock theater with the progressive band Genesis, Peter Gabriel went on to explore the confluence of third-world musical traditions and high-tech gadgetry.

ROUNDABOUT:

PROGRESSIVE ROCK

As psychedelia receded into hard rock, smooth soul, and true confessions, it appeared that rock and roll's spirit of adventure had died with the Woodstock generation. It wasn't dead, though; it simply retired to the woodshed in search of ways to break free of its own restrictions. During the early seventies, a plethora of British bands such as Emerson, Lake & Palmer, King Crimson, Yes, Genesis, and Gentle Giant, plus the Dutch group Focus ("Hocus Pocus," 1973)—not to mention the U.K. progressive underground of Soft Machine, Gong, Hatfield & the North, and Henry Cow—took it upon themselves to test the limits. They performed side-long epics that pushed standards of manual dexterity, formal rigor, and sheer imagination to new heights, while enlarging the scope of rock lyrics to encompass lofty themes such as Eastern religions and existentialism.

The progressive rockers played with an unflinching confidence that many critics mistook for pomposity. Although they could indeed be pompous, they could also be dazzling, sublime, and uncompromising, qualities missing elsewhere in music during the seventies. Over a few years, the progressive groups amassed a body of work that has permanently widened the musical and literary purview of rock and roll.

British Progressive Rock: The Nice, The Moody Blues, King Crimson, ELP, Yes, and Genesis

As early as 1967, organist Keith Emerson and the Nice had been working toward a fusion of classical forms and jazz improvisation with the power of a rock and roll band. Not only did they conceive their own compositions in terms of themes and movements, they also played revved-up versions of the classics, occasionally with a full orchestra in tow. The Nice made headlines with their onstage antics—they were banned from the Royal Albert Hall for burning an American flag onstage during their rendition of Leonard Bernstein's song from *West Side Story,* "America"—but their music remained obscure.

The Moody Blues managed to popularize the pairing of rock band and orchestra with their best-selling protoprogressive concept album, *Days of Future Passed* (1968), recorded with the London Symphony. "Nights in White Satin," the single, took a few years to catch on; the song was far more popular when it was re-released in 1972, as progressive rock was reaching its apex. "Nights" also featured a new electronic instrument, the mellotron, which offered simulations of orchestral instruments. (The mellotron had made its debut in 1967 providing flutes for the Beatles' "Strawberry Fields Forever.") A fascination with electronic gizmos of all sorts became one of the hallmarks of the progressive style.

The new instrument also turned up in King Crimson's early efforts. Their debut, *In the Court of the Crimson King* (1969), used lush washes of mellotron to such dramatic effect that it launched a raft of records employing the so-called "sweeping mellotron sound," including early efforts by Yes and Genesis. Crimson's trump card, though, was leader Robert Fripp. An eccentric genius of the electric guitar, Fripp propelled his instrument into the stratosphere on the fractured twelve-bar blues interlude of "Twentieth Century Schizoid Man." The song featured a deliberately distorted vocal performance by lead singer and bass player Greg Lake.

Lake left King Crimson in 1970 to join Keith Emerson in the first progressive-rock supergroup, Emerson, Lake & Palmer. Fueled by Emerson's inventive musicianship and spectacularly fleet fingers, the trio updated the blues-rock power trio format for high-tech keyboards, and set new standards for instrumental prowess in rock and roll. (Both Jimi Hendrix and the Guess Who's Randy Bachman were approached to fill out the group, but declined.) The highlight of ELP's live set was Mussorgsky's virtuoso piano epic, *Pictures at an Exhibition,* spiked with a shot of rhythm and blues. On the other hand, like their blues-rock forebears, ELP released singles that were paragons of catchy simplicity, including "Lucky Man" (1970) and "From the Beginning" (1972). Both songs offered tasty Emerson solos on yet another newfangled keyboard instrument, the synthesizer.

While Emerson was still fronting the Nice, a London band called Yes served as the opening act at Cream's final show in 1968. On their eponymous debut album the following year, Yes elevated

songs by the Beatles and the Byrds into triumphant cantatas. Lead singer Jon Anderson's choir-
boy voice provided a distinctive musical focus, and
with the addition in 1971 of virtuoso Steve Howe
on guitar and Rick Wakeman on electronic keyboards, the band became something of a rock and
roll orchestra. Over the next three years, they produced some of progressive rock's definitive
moments, including the hit single "Roundabout"
(1971) and the albums *Close to the Edge* (1972)
and *Relayer* (1974).

Genesis went through a similar development,
having formed at Charterhouse Public School during the mid-sixties. Although an album of early
demos has appeared, their first official release was
Trespass in 1969. That album shows them setting
imaginative fantasy stories to music in the dramatic manner that would sustain them well
beyond the double-LP rock opera, *The Lamb Lies
Down on Broadway* (1974). With that album, lead
singer Peter Gabriel left to become one of the premier art rockers of the eighties. Meanwhile, the
group continued with erstwhile drummer Phil
Collins in front, eventually achieving the greatest
commercial success of any progressive band.
Collins, of course, rose to superstardom in his own
right, as well as contributing some of the best
material on Genesis albums such as *Invisible
Touch* (1986).

American
Progressive Rock:
Frank Zappa

While the British progressives created a common
style combining the values of eighteenth-century
classical music with rock and roll, American progressives have tended to work in isolation, forging
idiosyncratic statements that would be unlikely to
develop into a movement. Although they can't be
called progressive rockers, rugged individualists
such as the Residents and Captain Beefheart illus-
trate this peculiar Stateside tendency. In terms of
rock and roll progressivism, the best example is
Frank Zappa.

Zappa's early West-Coast band, the Blackouts
(which included Captain Beefheart), made a splash
when it was revealed that the moaning female voice
on one of their racy recordings was actually that of a
minor. The incident landed Zappa in jail and set the
tone for much of his later work.

His ground-breaking first album with the Mothers of Invention, *Freak Out*—the first two-LP set
ever released by a rock act—appeared in 1966. It
was an entirely original work that marked Zappa as

© Gary Gershoff/Retna Ltd.

rock's foremost satirist, social critic, and smart-ass;
the set was a mind-boggling collage of electronic
noise, dissonant orchestral rambling, and edgy pop
spoof. The extraordinarily prolific composer cranked
out dozens of albums in the coming years, scoring
hits with snide jibes at social trends such as "Jewish
American Princess" (1979) and "Valley Girl"
(1982), sung by Zappa's perky daughter Moon Unit.
(Incidentally, Moon is now one of MTV's most popular VJs, while son Dweezil is a respected recording
artist in his own right).

More recently, Zappa has secured his place in
the history of rock guitar with a monumental *Shut
Up and Play Yer Guitar,* and has been an outspoken
critic of censorship efforts by the likes of the Parents Music Resource Center. In 1986 Zappa testi-
fied before Congressional censorship hearings,
along with Dee Snider of Twisted Sister. Needless
to say, our esteemed representatives are not likely
to invite Zappa back any time soon.

Progressive Rock
and the Mass
Audience: Jethro Tull

Progressive rock initially offered itself as an alternative to the banalities of the mainstream, but the
extraordinary musicianship of its major exponents
couldn't help but be noticed. The best of the British progressive bands became staples of AOR during the late seventies and early eighties. The way
had been paved by "progressive" hard-pop groups
such as Kansas and Queen. When they ran out of
steam, their more creative and energetic progeni-
tors stepped into the void, settling for a watered-
down version of their former glory.

At least one band, Jethro Tull, seemed to genuinely straddle the fence. Formed in 1968, the
group originally played jazzy blues. Charismatic
leader Ian Anderson injected a folkish flavor as the
group racked up a number of melodic hard-rock
hits. The *Aqualung* album in 1971 had a heavier
sound, but found Anderson attempting a side-long
suite of songs elucidating his views on organized
religion. From there, Tull jumped headlong into
dizzying album-length compositions, *Thick as a
Brick* (1972) and *Passion Play* (1973), with elaborate live shows to match. *War Child* (1974) marked
a return to tuneful, folk-influenced hard rock, but
subsequent albums bear the filigreed mark of
Jethro Tull's progressive days.

Today, progressive pioneers Yes and Genesis
are more popular than ever before, while ELP
re-forms in a slightly different configuration every
few years. Unfortunately, progressivism seemed to
have played itself out by the mid-seventies, and for
the most part their music has devolved into hard
pop. Although it lives on in revivalist bands such as
England's Marillion, the progressive-rock phoenix
is unlikely to rise from the ashes.

**Opposite: One of the most durable of the British progressive rock
groups, Genesis. Center: Rock and roll iconoclast and funnyman
Frank Zappa.**

FUTURE SHOCK:
TECHNOPOP/TECHNODANCE

The progressive rockers relied on new technology that more traditional rockers regarded with deep suspicion. But for all of their synthesizers, sequencers, and mellotrons, the progressives were as interested in a great guitar riff as anyone else. The technopop school, on the other hand, took high technology as a starting point. These bands traded their guitars and drums for a wall of knobs and dials, blinking LEDs, and computer screens.

Technopop celebrated the subservience of humanity to the machine. Both the synthesizer's pristine textures and the sequencer's mechanical precision signified the superficiality and lockstep conformity of modern life. But often there was also a triumph of human values in the music, a sense of mastering technology and turning it toward the simple joy of making rock and roll.

Kraftwerk and Giorgio Moroder

Kraftwerk (German for "power plant") are the pioneers of the technopop school. Formed in Dusseldorf in 1968, the duo of Ralf Hutter and Florian Schneider grew out of a need to build an aesthetic from the ground up after the cultural and spiritual devastation of World War II. They kicked off a distinguished line of electronic duos that includes the Pet Shop Boys, Orchestral Manoeuvres in the Dark, and the Communards.

At the time, the only electronic instruments available were tape recorders and test-tone oscillators. Kraftwerk incorporated early synthesizers as they became available, releasing three relatively unsuccessful albums in Germany only. (Another German synth outfit, Tangerine Dream, set out at the same time, but tended more toward dreamy new age landscapes.)

By their fourth album, *Autobahn* (1975), Kraftwerk's sound was uniquely high-tech but familiar, rendering the basic elements of rock and roll in cold, lifeless sonorities and deadpan vocal chants. The title track, filling an entire LP side, depicted an excursion along the German superhighway to an incessant robotic beat. Whittled down to three minutes for single release, it was a surprise radio hit in North America.

The same year, Donna Summer's "Love to Love You Baby," with its percolating electronic beat, was a smash disco hit. After touring Europe with the cast of *Hair*, Summer had settled in Germany, where she met producer Giorgio Moroder. Moroder, inspired by Kraftwerk's innovations, created moody disco epics that included both European romanticism and high-tech alienation. Moroder's success, in turn, pushed Kraftwerk into the disco limelight. "Trans-Europe Express" (1977) was a dance-floor smash and by far their biggest hit.

The British Technopop Wave

Meanwhile, technopop caught on in Britain. Drum machines and synthesizers of ever more sophisticated design were becoming plentiful and simpler to operate, making them attractive to any group that wanted to set themselves apart from the crowd. The late seventies saw the formation of Gary Numan's Tubeway Army ("Cars," 1978), one-hit wonder M ("Pop Muzik," 1978), consistent U.K. hitmakers Orchestral Manoeuvres in the Dark ("Enola Gay," 1980), Ultravox ("Vienna," 1981), and Human League ("Don't You Want Me," 1981).

Human League's approach, in particular, combined lyrical wit with catchy tunes and danceable rhythms, and proved irresistible to the pop market. "Don't You Want Me," Number One on both sides of the Atlantic, ushered in a full-scale technopop onslaught.

Synthesizers in the Mainstream

In 1982, artists of all stripes embraced electronics. Motown giant Marvin Gaye produced *Midnight Love,* yielding the suave electro-smash "Sexual Healing." Stepping even further out of character, Neil Young leaped into the twenty-first century with *Trans,* which gave a high-tech gloss to his usually blistering rock and roll. Doomy punk rockers Joy Division, having lost their leader Ian Curtis to suicide in 1980, rose from the ashes as New Order, offering perky punk disco hits such as "Blue Monday." Newcomers Soft Cell had a huge pop hit with a sparse medley of "Tainted Love" and the Supremes' "Where Did Our Love Go," while Afrika Bambaataa combined Kraftwerk and streetwise rap in the futuristic "Planet Rock."

The Disco Connection: Technodance

The earliest technopop hits of Kraftwerk and Gary Numan were eminently danceable, and discos discovered and appropriated them in a flash. In the aftermath of disco's golden age, a harder version of technopop arose to dominate dance clubs in cities throughout the world, represented by groups such as Scritti Politti, Art of Noise, Falco, Bronski Beat, and the Communards. The Pet Shop Boys' hypnotic synths, bottom-heavy beat, and deliberately wry delivery brought them a string of hits that included "West End Girls" (1985), "Opportunities" (1986), and "It's a Sin" (1987, legally confirmed as a plagiarized version of Cat Stevens' "Wild World").

The Boys refused to perform live until 1991, when they took a multimedia technopop opera on the road in America. The same year, they teamed up with members of New Order and the Smiths under the moniker Electronic, the first technopop supergroup.

As the nineties move into full gear, it's clear that Kraftwerk's high-tech groove has gathered unstoppable momentum. Bands like Information Society—oddly enough, one of the only American techno groups in history—suggest that technopop stands at a crossroads, facing dance pop, rap, house, industrial, and even third-world hybrids. As these styles converge, the result is bound to be an apocalyptic foot-stomping technology-intensive party music that transcends current boundaries of rock and dance, pop and punk, black and white: the music of Marshall McLuhan's global village.

Once electronic instruments became ubiquitous, they were much less interesting in and of themselves, and the technopop genre's egghead identity began to diffuse. Much of technopop's energy was siphoned off by the burgeoning "new romantic" movement spearheaded by Duran Duran, Culture Club, and Depeche Mode. Depeche Mode founder Vince Clark left the group in 1981 to form Yaz (called Yazoo in the U.K.), and then Erasure ("Chains of Love," 1988).

Having contributed electronic textures to hardpop Foreigner's smash "Feels Like the First Time" (1977), Thomas Dolby made a momentous splash with the delightfully quirky "She Blinded Me With

Science" in 1983. Howard Jones turned in a poppier take on technology with his smash album *Human Lib* in 1984, which placed two singles, "New Song" and "What Is Love," on the charts, and launched Jones on a long-lasting career.

Opposite: Scritti Politti delivers snappy technodance hits. Above: The Pet Shop Boys racked up a string of hits through the late 1980s without ever having performed live.

OVERKILL:
HEAVY METAL

Born in the crucible of blues-psychedelic-glitter-hard rock during the seventies, heavy metal is like the generic monster of grade-B horror flicks—it never dies. The blues always was the Devil's music, and many an early bluesman felt that he might sell his soul for the talent and stamina necessary to play the music; legend has it that the great Delta guitarist Robert Johnson did just that. But as the sixties skidded into history, it was Ozzy Osbourne's Black Sabbath that transmuted this occult connection into a metaphor for liberation from the cosmic

punishment of being teenaged and male. The Frankenstein they unleashed far outlived anyone's expectations and threatens to stalk the earth for a long time to come.

Along with ghoulish images of (teen) victory over (adult) oppression, heavy metal offers a sense of belonging rivalled only by punk—a dress code (big hair, black leather, and black tee-shirts emblazoned with the logo of the wearer's favorite band), a code of social values (anti-authoritarianism, misogyny, homophobia, and the party imperative), and the mass ritual of the stadium concert. Metal was the first rock style to make teenagers feel comfortable with their gangly, acne-splotched unattractiveness, rather than oppressed by it. Like Peter Pan, metal *can't* grow up, which may explain its inability to elicit sympathy from adult rock critics.

Alloys

Virtually ignored by radio and the press, heavy metal has thrived on the soil of dozens of countries, making it one of the few truly international rock subgenres. Apart from scores of groups from the United States and the United Kingdom, there are megastars AC/DC from Australia, Krokus from Switzerland, the Scorpions and Accept from Germany, Loudness from Japan, and even East-bloc metal bands, each offering few distinguishing characteristics from a musical point of view.

And yet substyles do exist within the metal community. Saxon, Dokken, Krokus, and Accept offer a Gothic, leather-clad version, while Motley Crüe and Twisted Sister dish out Kiss-derived glitter metal. Top-Forty fixtures such as Aerosmith,

Van Halen, Bon Jovi, and Def Leppard might be considered pop metal. Not to mention two recent underground permutations, death metal and speed metal.

But metal, in all its monochromatic variety, is rooted in a long tradition. The first use of the term appears to have been Steppenwolf's 1968 anthem "Born to be Wild," which describes its biker-gang heroes as swathed in "heavy metal thunder." After Black Sabbath's pioneering efforts in 1969, a number of bands helped to differentiate metal from the prevailing styles of blues-based hard rock. Foremost among them were Judas Priest, AC/DC, and Blue Oyster Cult.

Judas Priest and AC/DC

Arriving on the scene well after Sabbath, Deep Purple, Uriah Heep, and others, Judas Priest tended to be regarded as an anachronism when British vocalist Rob Halford formed the band in 1973. But the band was dedicated, refusing to change with the times as British rock became more elaborate and soft around the middle. Dressing in leather and chains and turning in muscular performances, the group finally hit in 1979 with *Killing Machine* (called *Hell Bent for Leather* in North America). Poised on the edge of a commercial breakthrough, Priest was in a prime position to spearhead the wave of British metallurgists that crashed in 1980.

The British metal wave of 1980 swept in Def Leppard, Iron Maiden, Saxon, the Scorpions, Ozzy Osbourne and his band (featuring the late lamented guitar virtuoso Randy Rhoads), and Whitesnake (comprising remnants of Deep Purple). It also gave a push to an Australian group that had been topping the charts in their own country since 1975, AC/DC. Driven by guitarist Angus Young's buzz-saw guitar and school-boy-prankster stage getup, AC/DC virtually put Australia on the rock and roll map.

Opposite: Judas Priest. Left: Ozzy Osbourne.

Stage Names

Gary Anderson	Gary "U.S." Bonds
Marc Bell	Marky Ramone
Marvin Lee Aday	Meatloaf
Michael Barratt	Shakin' Stevens
Richie Beau	Richie Ramone
Anna Mae Bullock	Tina Turner
Chester Burnette	Howlin' Wolf
Jon Bongiovi	Jon Bon Jovi
Mary Christine Brockert	Teena Marie
Madonna Louise Veronica Ciccone	Madonna
Douglas Coldin	Dee Dee Ramone
Ingram Cecil Conner	Gram Parsons
Vincent Eugene Craddock	Gene Vincent
John Cummings	Johnny Ramone
Tiffany Renee Darwish	Tiffany
Sandy Denton	Pepa (Salt-N-Pepa)
John Henry Deutschendorf, Jr.	John Denver
Michael Diamond	Mike D (Beastie Boys)
Dion DiMucci	Dion
Daryl Dragon	The Captain (the Captain & Tennille)
August Darnell	Kid Creole (Kid Creole & the Coconuts)
Reginald Kenneth Dwight	Elton John
Cass Elliott	Mama Cass
Tommy Erdelyi	Tommy Ramone
Sheila Escovedo	Sheila E.
Dave Evans	The Edge (U2)

Vincent Furnier	Alice Cooper
Paul Gadd	Gary Glitter
Steven Georgiou	Cat Stevens
Stuart Goddard	Adam Ant
Kennedy Gordy	Rockwell
Peter Greenbaum	Peter Green (Fleetwood Mac)
Richard Griffin	Professor Griff (Public Enemy)
Paul Hewson	Bono Vox (U2)
Charles Hardin Holley	Buddy Holly
Sam Hopkins	Lightnin' Hopkins
Adam Horovitz	King Adrock (Beastie Boys)
Jeffrey Hyman	Joey Ramone
Oshea Jackson	Ice Cube
Cheryl James	Salt (Salt-N-Pepa)
David Robert Jones	David Bowie
David Johansen	Buster Poindexter
Dennis Leigh	John Foxx (Ultravox)
John Lydon	Johnny Rotten (Sex Pistols)
Rudy Martinez	? (?Question Mark & the Mysterians)
Elias McDaniel	Bo Diddley
Darryl McDaniels	DMC (Run-DMC)
Ron McKernan	Pigpen (the Grateful Dead)
Declan McManus	Elvis Costello
Tammi Montgomery	Tammi Terrell
McKinley Morganfield	Muddy Waters
Steveland Morris	Stevie Wonder
Prince Rogers Nelson	Prince

Peter Noone	Herman (Herman's Hermits)
Taco Ockerse	Taco
George Alan O'Dowd	Boy George (Culture Club)
James Jewel Osterberg	Iggy Pop
Kurtis Ousley	King Curtis
Dana Owens	Queen Latifah
Georgious Panayatiou	George Michael
Lawrence Parker	KRS-ONE (Boogie Down Productions)
Benjamin Franklin Peay	Brook Benton
Richard Wayne Penniman	Little Richard
Malcolm John Rebennack, Jr.	Dr. John
J.P. Richardson	The Big Bopper
Carleton Ridenhour	Chuck D (Public Enemy)
Dee Dee Roper	Spinderella (Salt-N-Pepa)
Cherilyn Sarkisian	Cher
William Royce Scaggs	Boz Scaggs
Joseph Simmons	Run (Run-DMC)
James Todd Smith	LL Cool J
Tony Smith	Tone Lōc, short for Tony Loco
Chris St. John	Chris Cross (Ultravox)
Gordon Sumner	Sting (the Police)
Don Van Vliet	Captain Beefheart
Kurtis Walker	Kurtis Blow
Charles Westover	Del Shannon
Adam Yauch	MCA (Beastie Boys)
Robert Allen Zimmerman	Bob Dylan

AC/DC's 1979 effort, *Highway to Hell,* was hailed as a metal classic. Tragically, lead shrieker Bon Scott died during a drinking binge soon after the album was released. But the group came out rocking the following year with the searing *Back in Black,* an aural orgy of wink-wink lasciviousness featuring Scott soundalike Brian Johnson. The album turned into one of the first metal best-sellers, and is memorialized in *Rolling Stone* magazine's *The 100 Greatest Albums of the Eighties.*

Blue Oyster Cult

If AC/DC represents metal's puerile side, Blue Oyster Cult were the intellectuals of the genre. From the start, the Long Island quintet set about creating a unique iconography and mythos; rather than comic-book superheroes, theirs suggested a sinister political conspiracy of international scope revolving around the occult.

Three excellent albums featuring cryptic lyrics (with occasional contributions by punk poet Patti Smith) and the guitar gymnastics of Donald "Buck Dharma" Roeser failed to attract much attention. The fourth, *Agents of Fortune,* yielded the group's first hit in 1976. It was a sweetly rendered ode to suicide called "(Don't Fear) The Reaper." Less metallic than most modern metal, BOC's contribution has been eclipsed as the genre's posture has become increasingly extreme.

Motley Crüe and American Metal c. 1983

A new wave of American metal rolled in like thunder with entrepreneur Steve Wozniak's "Woodstock for the Eighties," the 1983 US Festival, which featured a special day of metal acts. The Festival introduced groups from various local scenes, including Ratt and Quiet Riot from L.A., Zebra from New Orleans, and Twisted Sister from New York (who had been smothering their faces with makeup ever since the demise of the New York Dolls). One of the most successful groups from this brat pack were Motley Crüe.

The Crüe burst out of L.A.'s mousse-and-spandex metal scene in 1981. "We wanted to be the loudest and grossest band in the history of rock. We'd do anything to get attention," preened bass player Nikki Sixx, explaining the group's demonic glitter image—stopping just short of Kiss—and anti-authoritarian pose. After releasing a first album consisting of early demos, Sixx and friends struck platinum with *Shout at the Devil* in 1983.

Tragedy struck when lead vocalist Vince Neil was involved in an alcohol-related car accident that left one of his passengers dead, but the group's raucous spirit remained untempered. The platinum *Theatre of Pain* (1984), though, did include an anti-driving-while-intoxicated statement on the cover, perhaps as part of Neil's debt to society. Aside from a third platinum album, *Girls, Girls, Girls* (1987), Motley Crüe is distinguished by their celebrity wives: Prince's ex-consort Vanity wears Sixx's ring, while drummer Tommy Lee is married to actress Heather Locklear.

Pop Metal

Heavy metal is an anomaly in the record industry: It sells huge numbers of albums without the benefit of hit singles. By and large, metal doesn't produce hit singles at all. When it does, generally speaking, the music is pop metal.

There's a fine line between the tuneful pop metal of Van Halen and hard pop by, say, Foreigner. But the distinction isn't arbitrary. Van Halen, like Def Leppard and Bon Jovi, emphasizes putting on a dazzling show, having a ball, and generally being as outrageous as possible, while the hard-pop bands are concerned with putting across a hit single. The prototype pop-metal band is Aerosmith, who hail from Boston.

Aerosmith

Aerosmith appropriated the show-off licks and bawdy subject matter of groups like the Stones, the Yardbirds, and Mountain, infusing them with the sizzling energy and gut-level punch of heavy metal (plus a touch of smirking locker-room humor). It took three years for their first single, the wistful ballad "Dream on," to take off. But once it did, Aerosmith was flying high. "Walk This Way" followed, and their second album, *Toys in the Attic* (1975), stayed on the charts for two years.

Although the group didn't reach Number One again for more than a decade (with "Dude Looks Like a Lady" in 1987), they remained extraordinarily popular in the interim. Their rap-rock crossover version of "Walk This Way," in collaboration with Run-DMC, demonstrated the continuing appeal of their music and made explicit the historical connection between hard rock and rap. Aerosmith's 1989 album, *Pump,* showed the band still going strong (albeit with a cleaned-up image) for the nineties.

Van Halen

Van Halen took Aerosmith's approach light-years further, thanks to the macho charm of front man David Lee Roth, and to the stunning originality of guitarist Eddie Van Halen. (One of the most influential guitarists since Hendrix, Eddie pioneered a two-handed fret-tapping style that has been assimilated by virtually every electric guitarist since.) Gene Simmons of Kiss financed the demo tapes that got Van Halen their record contract. The band's first single, a cover of the Kinks' "You Really Got Me" (1978), took the accompanying album to triple platinum, and several hit singles followed, including "Dance the Night Away" (1979) and the phenomenally popular "Jump" (1984).

David Lee Roth left soon thereafter, going on to make hits such as his ebullient cover of the Beach Boys "California Girls" (1985), while Van Halen recruited Sammy Hagar to take his place. Their first album with Hagar, *5150* (1986), was their biggest seller yet. *OU812* followed in 1988, but suggested a lack of energy that has been reinforced by Van Halen's inactivity in the years since.

Bon Jovi

Into the breach stepped a young band from New Jersey, Bon Jovi. Possessing neither the originality, the songwriting smarts, nor the instrumental prowess of Van Halen, the group nonetheless managed to take the world by storm with the release of their eponymous debut in 1984. Their second album, *7800 Fahrenheit* (1985) found them consolidating their gains, and with *Slippery When Wet* (1986), they achieved genuine superstar status. "You Give Love a Bad Name" and "Livin' on a Prayer," the album's singles, carried the album to platinum sales eight times over. The follow-up, *New Jersey* (1988), continued Bon Jovi's success with "I'll Be There for You," and the following year, leader Jon Bon Jovi scored the film *Young Guns II,* releasing the score as *Blaze of Glory* (1990).

Bands like Bon Jovi, Van Halen, and Tesla demonstrate that metal can reach a broader audience simply by softening its rough edges, while groups such as the Scorpions, Iron Maiden, and Queensryche keep the tradition alive. But current trends suggest that metal is moving in another direction. The music is getting rougher, faster, wilder, and more confrontational.

The most promising development is bands like Jane's Addiction, who in their short association made arty funk-metal that defied classification, and yet inspired huge airplay and record sales. Meanwhile, renegade subgenres such as speed metal and funk metal, not to mention local scenes such as Seattle's early-nineties retro-metal groups, suggest that heavy metal now carries the banner as the uncompromising music of white rockers. Heavy metal isn't for kids any more. It may just be the vanguard of rock and roll.

Rock and Roll Couples

Paula Abdul and John Stamos (actor)
Nikolas Ashford and Valerie Simpson (Ashford & Simpson)
David Bowie and Iman (model)
Jackson Browne and Daryl Hannah (actress)
Lindsey Buckingham and Stevie Nicks (both of Fleetwood Mac)
Exene Cervenka and John Doe (both of X)
Cher and Sonny Bono (Sonny & Cher)
Cher and Gregg Allman (the Allman Brothers)
Cher and Gene Simmons (Kiss)
Cher and Richie Sambora (Bon Jovi)
Cher and Eric Clapton
Eric Clapton and Patti Harrison (ex-wife of George Harrison)
Elvis Costello and Cait O'Riordan (the Pogues)
Bo Diddley and Lady Bo
The Captain & Tennille
Bob Dylan and Joan Baez
Brian Eno and Julie Christie (actress)
Bryan Ferry and Jerry Hall (model)
Peter Gabriel and Rosanna Arquette (actress)
Marvin Gaye and Tammi Terrell
Marvin Gaye and Anna Gordy (Berry Gordy's daughter)
Deborah Harry and Chris Stein (both of Blondie)
Michael Hutchence (INXS) **and Kylie Minogue**

Chrissie Hynde and Ray Davies (the Kinks)
Chrissie Hynde and Jim Kerr (Simple Minds)
Michael Jackson and Brooke Shields (actress)
Michael Jackson and Tatum O'Neal (actress)
Mick Jagger and Marianne Faithfull
Mick Jagger and Jerry Hall (model)
Billy Joel and Christie Brinkley (model)
Grace Jones and Dolph Lundgren (actor)
Lenny Kravitz and Lisa Bonet (actress)
Tommy Lee (Motley Crüe) **and Heather Locklear** (actress)
John Lennon and Yoko Ono
Madonna and Jellybean Benitez (remix engineer)
Madonna and Sean Penn (actor)
Madonna and Warren Beatty (actor)
Bob and Rita Marley (both of the Wailers)
Paul and Linda McCartney (Wings)
John and Christine McVie (both of Fleetwood Mac)
Joni Mitchell and Graham Nash (Crosby, Stills, Nash & Young)
Ric Ocasek (the Cars) **and Paulina Porizkova** (model)
Peaches and Herb
John and Michelle Phillips (both of the Mamas and the Papas)
Elvis and Priscilla Presley
Prince and Kim Basinger (actress)
Prince and Sheena Easton
Keith Richards and Patti Hansen (model)

Linda Ronstadt and Jerry Brown (politician)
Paul Simon and Carrie Fisher (actress)
Paul Simon and Edie Brickell
Nikki Sixx (Motley Crüe) **and Vanity** (Vanity 6)
Grace Slick and Paul Kantner (both of the Jefferson Airplane/Starship)
Patti Smith and Sam Shepard (playwright)
Patti Smith and Fred "Sonic" Smith (MC5)
Patti Smith and Allen Lanier (Blue Oyster Cult)
Phil Spector (producer) **and Veronica "Ronnie" Bennett** (the Ronettes)
Bruce Springsteen and Patti Scialfa (backup vocalist)
Dave Stewart and Annie Lennox (both of Eurythmics)
Rod Stewart and Britt Eklund (actress)
Rod Stewart and Kelly Emberg (model)
Rod Stewart and Rachel Hunter (model)
Stephen Stills (Crosby, Stills, Nash & Young) **and Judy Collins**
Ringo Starr and Barbara Bach (actress)
James Taylor and Carly Simon
Richard and Linda Thompson
Ike and Tina Turner
Eddie Van Halen and Valerie Bertinelli (actress)
Sid Vicious (the Sex Pistols) **and Nancy Spungen**
Tina Weymouth and Chris Frantz (both of Talking Heads)
Gay and Terry Woods (both of Steeleye Span, Terry of the Pogues)

Boasting both a swaggering front man and virtuoso guitar gymnastics, Van Halen set a new standard for pop metal.

Chapter Three

Punk Rock and Beyond

ANARCHY IN THE U.K.:

THE PUNK ROCK REVOLUTION

By the mid-seventies, rock and roll's potential as a moneymaker had been proven time and time again, and the industry was looking for big sales. An album was unlikely to be pressed without projected sales in the hundreds of thousands, and the major labels—now owned by multinational corporations—ensured such figures by maintaining a stranglehold on manufacturing, distribution, and promotion. Even artists seemed to be in on the scam, dishing out whatever seemed most likely to hit. The docile public, trained by cynical radio programmers and self-serving music critics, gobbled up whatever was offered: escapist disco, slick pop, or lumbering corporate rock. Rock and roll needed new blood.

Enter the punks. By and large, they were working-class kids, alienated by the spiritual emptiness of their culture, who felt they had nothing to lose by posing themselves in direct opposition to society. Anti-bourgeois and anti-capitalist—anti-everything, in fact—they brought about something of a cultural revolution in New York and London during the late seventies, and changed the face of rock and roll.

Punk performances were deliberately confrontational and anarchic; musicians spat at the audience, mutilated themselves with glass and knives, damaged property, and encouraged the audience to do the same. Their fashion sense emphasized violence and degradation, with chains, razor blades, dog collars, and safety pins through flesh functioning as accessories. A do-it-yourself ethic prevailed: Anyone could play an instrument, anyone could be a star, anyone could say or do anything imaginable in the name of liberating rock and roll from its aging aristocracy. Though their rebellious populism was familiar, the apparent extremism of the punks was something entirely new.

© Stevenson/Retna Ltd.

Punk Roots

The musical forefathers of the punk movement don't share a single lineage, but represent the eccentric fringes of various scenes that had come and gone: the arty Velvet Underground, the glittering New York Dolls, the uncompromising MC5, and the acknowledged "Grandfather of Punk," Iggy Pop. Aside from raw, degenerate rock, Iggy Pop put across an intense version of the rock and roll anti-hero persona with his late-sixties band, the Stooges. Another punk precursor was Jonathan Richman and the Modern Lovers, whose 1974 classic *The Modern Lovers* set Richman's everyman philosophizing over a dark Velvets-inspired grind. Both Iggy's and Richman's debuts were produced by John Cale of the Velvet Underground.

New York Punk: CBGB and the Ramones

Although the most outrageous expressions of punk appeared in England, the first signs that a revolution was at hand surfaced in New York City, in a hole-in-the-wall club called CBGB (which actually stands for country, blue grass, and blues). The scene that brought Patti Smith and Talking Heads to national prominence was in its infancy in 1974, when four suburban Brooklynites came to CBGB looking for a place to play. Naming themselves after Paul McCartney's stage name during an early pre-Beatlemania tour (Paul Ramon), they called themselves the Ramones.

They couldn't play or sing, but they had an irresistible pose as Bowery hoodlums and an off-beat sense of humor. More significantly, the group's musical restraint was something of an innovation: no solos, no introductions (save Joey Ramone's invariable "One, two, three, four!"), and no songs longer than two minutes. Performing high-octane odes to teen alienation like "I Wanna Sniff Some Glue," they were booed off of the stage during their first gig, opening for Johnny Winter. But when they landed a record deal in the spring of 1976, record companies started signing New York bands in droves.

British Punk: the Sex Pistols

When the Ramones toured Britain in 1976, the United Kingdom was in a bleak state. Inflation was rising 12 percent annually. Unemployment was rising at about double that rate, leaving teenagers with little to do but contemplate their predicament. In Britain, the amateurism, irony, and pessimism of the New York scene took on overt sociopolitical implications, offering a language in which the nation's disaffected youth could express their frustrations. By the end of the year, punk had exploded across the land in the form of the Gang of Four, the Buzzcocks, the Damned, Siouxsie & the Banshees, Sham 69, Generation X (featuring Billy Idol), and dozens of other bands.

But a British version of punk was in the works even before the Ramones arrived. Malcolm McLaren, the wily Englishman who had managed the New York Dolls just before their demise, resolved in 1975 to bring the New York spirit to London. Rounding up four of the grubbiest, most obnoxious teenagers he could find, he handed them instruments and dubbed them the Sex Pistols.

Opposite: The Sex Pistols revitalized rock and roll through the punk aesthetic of amateurism, antisocial behavior, and crash-and-burn tactics.

McLaren conceived his creation as the antithesis of rock and roll at the time. Rather than virtuosic, they were blatantly unskilled. Rather than glamorous glitter-rock dos, they wore tee-shirts and jeans, their hair short and spiked (a fashion pioneered by New York's Richard Hell). If nothing else, leader Johnny Rotten's sneer was the perfect antidote to Mick Jagger's come-hither looks. And to top it all off, they were irredeemably rude in public.

The history of the Sex Pistols is one of the great tragicomedies of modern times. Touted as the next big thing, they were signed by EMI Records in 1976, for which they reaped a £40,000 advance. Their first single, "Anarchy in the U.K.," however, was considered so offensive that employees at EMI's pressing plant refused to manufacture it. ("You don't sing about love to people on the dole," Rotten retorted.) When Rotten cussed out the host on a live TV show shortly thereafter, EMI dropped the Sex Pistols like a hot potato.

McLaren milked the publicity. A&M signed the group, providing an advance of £75,000, but got nervous and backed out virtually immediately. Next, Virgin stepped up with £50,000. They released "God Save the Queen" ("and her bloody fascist regime!") just in time to coincide with Queen Elizabeth's Silver Jubilee in 1977. As a result, the Pistols were banned by broadcasters and concert halls throughout the country. By the time their album, *Never Mind the Bollocks, Here's the Sex Pistols* appeared in 1977, public interest was so intense that it was a runaway best-seller.

As their reputation reached a peak in Britain, the Pistols made a deliberately suicidal move: They undertook a tour of the American South, where audiences were hardly prepared for punk rock. Concerts erupted into brawls as Rotten taunted listeners from the stage. On the night of their last U.S. show, he announced the group's breakup. Bass player Sid Vicious stayed behind in New York.

The group's denouement took a tragic turn when, in late 1978, Vicious was charged with the murder of his girlfriend, Nancy Spungen. Within four months, Vicious himself was found dead of a heroin overdose. The headlines seemed a fitting epitaph for the most overwhelmingly negative movement in the history of popular culture.

The Clash

For all the energy of the U.K. punk movement, the only group to achieve lasting success was the Clash. After their initial gig opening for the Sex Pistols, the group, led by the indefatigable Joe Strummer and Mick Jones, put out a series of highly acclaimed singles that melded a snarling punk approach with an effective pop sensibility. In contrast to punk's habitual disavowal of specific ideologies, the Clash struck an explicitly political stance, teaming up with London's chocolate-and-vanilla ska revival groups in a series of Rock Against Racism benefits.

Their third album, the urgent *London Calling* (1980), proved punk's relevance as a medium for social commentary even as the movement fell into disarray. *Rolling Stone* magazine rates it no less than the best album of the eighties. Further releases, notably the epic *Sandinista* (1981) and the more accessible *Combat Rock* (1982), widened their audience as well as their musical purview, which now embraced rap and dance-club funk. "Rock the Casbah," *Combat's* single, charted in both North America and the United Kingdom as the group toured with fledgling rap group Grandmaster Flash & the Furious Five and New York graffiti artist Futura 2000. Although the Clash carried on only until 1985 (Mick Jones went on to Big Audio Dynamite), their example proved that punk could evolve without losing its bite—a crucial lesson for the post-punk bands that followed.

Although it never caught on with the public—both the music and the posture were just far too radical—punk nonetheless ranks as one of the major developments in contemporary popular music. It is significant both as a grass-roots rebellion against manufactured culture and as an assertion of basic musical values in the face of an industry grown flabby with indulgence and pandering. The punks never intended to sound good. They only meant to shock listeners and industry mavens alike out of a sleep brought on by boredom and complacency. They were successful. Rock and roll is surely healthier for it.

PARALLEL LINES:
THE NEW WAVE

The upheaval of punk sent talent scouts running for the clubs even as it sent their bosses running for cover. Much of what they turned up was hardly punk. Rather, it was pop-oriented rock of one stripe or another. But under punk's pervasive influence, virtually all of it was a far cry from the sounds glutting the charts in 1976.

For one thing, the songs tended to be short and to the point. Their subject matter was either centered on traditional pop-song issues, often with an offbeat twist, or insistently left-field. The ensembles were usually stripped down to two guitars, bass, and drums. In addition, a vaguely intellectual touch of irony crept into just about everything.

Within those parameters, the music displayed immense variety, and it became known by the catch-all phrase "new wave." At their best, the new wavers unearthed taut, intelligent pop gems with wide appeal that nonetheless retained the energy and toughness of punk.

Most new wave bands were unabashed pop rockers, including Blondie, the Cars, Cyndi Lauper, the Go-Gos (featuring Belinda Carlisle), Cheap Trick, Nick Lowe, Squeeze, Ireland's Boomtown Rats (including Live Aid organizer Bob Geldof), Scotland's Big Country, and Men at Work from Australia. The rest divide fairly evenly between weirdos such as the B-52's and Devo (art rockers Talking Heads initially appeared to fall into this category), art rockers in pop clothing like the Police and the sadly underrated XTC, and angry young men and women, including Elvis Costello, Joe Jackson, Graham Parker & the Rumour, and the Pretenders. Contemporaries such as Culture Club were allied more closely with specific movements—in the Club's case, the new romantics—and owed far less to the punks.

Big-time new wavers Blondie, who reworked American Defense-era pop for the punk era.

Blondie

Blondie's self-titled debut in 1977 was among the first new-wave releases, a facile reworking of American Defense pop. From the start, the focus was on their lead vocalist. In peroxide-headed former Playboy Club bunny Deborah Harry, they had both a Marilyn Monroe look-alike and a girl-group sound alike. After two moderately successful albums, Blondie crossed over with *Parallel Lines* (1978), selling a whopping 20 million copies. The group's stylistic range took a quantum leap; the hits that followed include the Eurodisco smash "Heart of Glass" (1978), "Dreaming" (1979), "Call Me" (1980), and the rap tribute/spoof "Rapture" (1981).

By then, Harry was increasingly involved in solo records and acting. Suddenly, in 1982, guitarist (and Harry's beau) Chris Stein fell ill with a rare genetic disease. He was hospitalized for much of the next two years. With Harry staying by his side, Blondie disbanded.

The Police

If Blondie cut the path, the Police navigated it in a limousine. The Police deliberately applied punk principles to more complex musical materials. Comprising photogenic bass player Sting, drummer extraordinaire Stewart Copeland, and chameleon guitarist Andy Summers, the group scored their first time out with the reggae-based "Roxanne" in 1978. Although it was relatively crude, the song summed up their approach: reggae rhythms, catchy tunes, concise arrangements, and Sting's charismatic presence.

The highlights were many: "Message in a Bottle" (1979), "Don't Stand So Close to Me" (1980), "Every Little Thing She Does Is Magic" (1981), "Every Breath You Take" (1983), and "King of Pain" (1984). By the release of *Ghost in the Machine* (1982), their albums were guaranteed multiplatinum, and the group split to undertake solo projects. They were back the following year with the spectacular *Synchronicity*. Although the Police never formally disbanded, they have not recorded together since, and have announced no plans to do so. Sting, of course, has become one of the major stars of the nineties with his jazz-inflected solo projects.

Elvis Costello

Fronted by pretty boy Sting, the Police were destined for stardom. Elvis Costello, on the other hand, looked more like an accountant than a rock star. This nerdy pose worked in his favor at the start, though, when the new wave was riding on the coattails of punk's iconoclasm.

Costello's hard-hitting 1977 debut, *My Aim Is True,* depicted a man every bit as angry as Johnny Rotten, if more restrained and articulate. That he wasn't really a punk was suggested by the tender "Alison," covered by Linda Ronstadt the following year. Each new album found him discovering new styles and writing ever more subtle songs: *Get Happy* (1980) relived the glory days of Motown, *Almost Blue* (1981) delved into country, *Imperial Bedroom* (1982) presented a *Sgt. Pepper*ish musical phantasmagoria, while *Punch the Clock* (1984) delivered slick modern pop.

Costello has continued to turn out high-quality records into the nineties, but oddly, mass popularity continues to elude him. He shows no sign of slowing down, though, nor of standing in one place. Of the new wavers, he may well leave the finest body of work behind.

As the apolitical fallout from the punk movement, new wave has been criticized as socially irrelevant—a serious charge in the realm of pop art. If nothing else, the new wave proved punk's assertion that the music industry had become hopelessly out of shape and out of touch. But it achieved much more. Although the old rock formulas remained, the new wave opened the door to musicians in a number of styles that previously wouldn't have been commercially viable, infusing rock and roll with new blood and bringing some extraordinary talents to light. A good deal of the pop music that appeared between the demise of punk and the rise of rap has been, essentially, new wave. That's a lot of music that the world would not have wanted to miss.

© Steve Granitz/Retna Ltd.

Police front man Sting, whose distinctive voice and solid musicianship anchored one of the most satisfying new wave bands.

FABLES OF THE RECON- STRUCTION:

HARDCORE, POSTPUNK, POST NEW WAVE, AND INDUSTRIAL

Rock and roll is over, don't you understand? It's gone on for twenty-five years and it's got to be cancelled. The Pistols finished rock and roll; they were the last rock and roll band. It's finished now, done with.

Johnny Rotten, 1980

© Darlene Hammond/Archive Photos

After punk, rock and roll would never be the same. The punks co-opted the music's aggressive energy, effectively shouting down any band that dared to consider themselves rebellious without acknowledging the punk aesthetic. They also cast a suspicious light on rock professionalism in any form, so that any aspiration to slickness smelled like a return to the dreaded corporate-rock past. The immediate reaction, at least in North America, was hardcore.

Hardcore

Hardcore escalated the fury of British punk even as it adapted its subject matter to America's more comfortable circumstances. When the Sex Pistols spit in the eye of society-at-large, they were celebrating the commonality of downtrodden youth. The basis of hardcore, on the other hand, was deep, biting sarcasm borne of suburban affluence and boredom. The music was a full-throttle sonic barrage, virtually without melody or any sense of

restraint. It was faster than cars speeding on the L.A. freeway and as monolithic as the concrete embankments into which they might crash. The hardcores actually *were* what the punks pretended to be—totally alienated, spiritually moribund, beyond rational comprehension.

The preeminent hardcore band was Black Flag (sample lyric: "I wanna live/I wish I was dead"). The Flag was part of a thriving Los Angeles scene that included Flipper, the Angry Samoans, Fear, and hardcore jokers the Circle Jerks. Northern California was represented by the Dead Kennedys, fronted by Jello Biafra, who ran for mayor of San Francisco under the slogan "California Uber Alles." In Washington, D.C., an East-Coast hardcore movement sprang up around Minor Threat, Government Issue, and S.O.A. Canada's entry was D.O.A. from Vancouver.

Oddly enough, the genre's two transcendent groups, Husker Dü and the Minutemen, hailed from Minneapolis. Husker Dü evolved from classic hardcore into a metallic art band with a surprising pop sensibility. The introspective roar of their *Zen Arcade* (1984) earned it a spot in *Rolling Stone* magazine's *The 100 Greatest Albums of the*

Eighties. Equally noteworthy is the Minutemen's virtuosic forty-six-song masterpiece, *Double Nickels on the Dime* (1984). One of the great unsung bands of the eighties, they transmuted into Firehose with the tragic death of leader D. Boone in 1985.

Postpunk

As the initial energy behind punk inevitably began to wane, the punks themselves began staking out new territory. Sex Pistol Johnny Rotten, reverting to his original last name, Lydon, formed Public Image Ltd. as a more flexible vehicle for his strident brand of social criticism. Billy Idol ("Rebel Yell," 1985) left Generation X, finding that his thunderous voice and sneering upper lip were perfect

Postpunk's first superstars, U2, place the inspired amateurism of punk in a context of anthemic arena rock.

"designer punk" fodder for the mainstream's star-making machinery. Members of the Gang of Four, exploring folk and country-and-western roots, formed the Mekons. Even hardcore musicians sought a more expressive form, as when a member of Minor Threat formed Fugazi.

Meanwhile, scores of up-and-coming rockers turned their attention away from neat, tidy arrangements and catchy hooks. Instead, groups such as X, Camper Van Beethoven, the Pixies, Naked Raygun, and Soul Asylum (produced by members of Husker Dü), and U.K. bands including the Psychedelic Furs and the Jesus and Mary Chain ("April Skies," 1987) concerned themselves with preserving the music's youthful energy and spontaneity, as well as its relevance to listeners. Stripped-down and rough-hewn, the music of the postpunk bands is simple but rarely simplistic, aggressive but rarely confrontational, and usually of an intellectual bent.

Among the most inventive of the postpunk groups are the Replacements, who were local hardcore competition for Husker Dü when they first started playing in 1981. Led by songwriter Paul Westerberg, they quickly outstripped the limitations of hardcore to produce a stirring, lyrical body of songs that never loses sight of the punk spirit.

Big-Time Postpunk

Too idiosyncratic for the Top Forty, postpunk was initially the sole province of independent record labels. Postpunk bands tend to attract their audiences without the benefit of hit singles, picking up fans purely on the basis of outstanding albums, exciting live shows, and selective airplay.

Throughout the eighties, college radio stations united the cult followings of dozens of obscure groups, creating something akin to a mass audience apart from the mainstream. Of course, the major labels couldn't resist. Today, "alternative" rock and roll is big business, boosting talented postpunks such as U2, the Cure, and Sinead O'Connor into megastardom.

U2

Formed in the best punk tradition in Dublin in 1979, U2 began as a group of rank amateurs. (The cryptic quality of their name was intended to deflect inevitable comparisons with other bands.) Nonetheless, the group developed a loyal following in Ireland based on their unflagging energy and the charisma of front man Bono Vox.

U2's appearance at the Live Aid benefit in 1985 cemented their reputation internationally. *Joshua Tree* (1987) prompted a massive tour and an appearance on the cover of *Time* magazine, as "With You or Without You" and "I Still Haven't Found What I'm Looking For" climbed the charts on both sides of the Atlantic. In 1989, the *Rattle and Hum* record and feature film confirmed the group's superstar status and features guest appearances by Bob Dylan, B.B. King, and Brian Eno. If they keep at it, U2 is sure to be one of the major draws of the nineties; rumor has it that Bono's 1990 income was the largest in all of Ireland.

The Cure

Like U2, the Cure began squarely in the punk spirit, but with a few feet of existentialist distance. Their 1978 debut, "Killing an Arab" (based on *The Stranger* by Albert Camus), raised unjust accusations of bigotry and set the dark, despairing tone of later releases. Playing with savage intensity behind vocalist Robert Smith's anguished wail, the group steadily acquired a cult following.

In 1982, drummer Lol Tolhurst switched to keyboards, and the group began to expand its palette. The sprawling *Kiss Me, Kiss Me, Kiss Me* appeared in 1987, a dizzying array of songs set in an immense, echoing ambiance. It sent "Just Like Heaven" into the charts and heralded the Cure's mature period. Although they have yet to score a top hit in North America (or, for that matter, a Number One in Britain), the Cure's popularity continues to grow along with their music.

Sinead O'Connor

From the moment she stepped before the public eye with *The Lion and the Cobra* in 1988, Sinead O'Connor has been a rock and roll icon. Certainly, part of the reason lies in her striking appearance: Possessed of innocent eyes and delicate features, her conventional beauty is undercut by a severely cropped crew cut.

But what makes O'Connor so attractive is the attitude of commitment she brings to her work. She refused to appear on *Saturday Night Live* when it turned out that misogynist comedian Andrew Dice Clay was scheduled to host the show. (It seems to be worth noting, though, that her feminist sensitivities didn't stop her from appearing on the *MTV Video Awards* show with archsexist rappers 2 Live Crew.) Later, with the United States at war in Iraq, she refused to play at the Garden State Arts Center if the national anthem was used to open the show, earning snide comments from none other than Frank Sinatra.

All of which wouldn't amount to much if she weren't among the most compelling talents to emerge during the postpunk era. O'Connor's Prince-penned hit, "Nothing Compares 2 U" (1990), proved her a commanding vocalist. Blending punk, hip-hop, art-rock, and Celtic folk influences, she fashions musical statements that are as personal as her performances are heartfelt. In an age dominated by cynical bids for fame (or, just as often, simply for laughs), Sinead O'Connor offers both riveting music and a refreshingly honest, soul-bearing persona.

Post New Wave

If punk revitalized rock and roll by channeling its rebellious tendencies, punk's dominant offshoot, new wave, left behind a renewed appreciation for straight-ahead, no-frills musicianship built on a base of British Invasion-era pop rock. American groups such as the Meat Puppets, the Feelies, the Violent Femmes, and the Fleshtones play melodic post New Wave that jingle-jangles with a nostalgic sense of purpose. Athens, Georgia, hosts a vigorous scene led by R.E.M.

R.E.M. and The Smiths

The members of R.E.M. dropped out of college in order to make their first single in 1982, which breaks the classic rock and roll pattern only insofar as they went to college in the first place. But the refined, literate approach they take to their otherwise murky sound confirms them as one of the smartest groups around. Perhaps most impressive, they've managed to become one of America's top bands without alienating their grass-roots following.

Like vintage Byrds, early R.E.M. emphasized texture above all else. As the title of their debut album *Murmur* (1983) suggests, Michael Stipe's lyrics are often indecipherable. *Document* (1987) landed the group on the cover of *Rolling Stone* with a headline proclaiming them "the best band in America." They never looked back. With a Number One album, *Out of Time* (1991), that featured cameos by KRS-1 of Boogie Down Productions and Kate Pierson of the B-52s, R.E.M. remains one of the brightest lights in the charts.

Although they never made a great impact in North America, the Smiths were one of the great British underground bands of the eighties. Piping tunes that were optimistically uptempo and hook-laden, lead vocalist Steven Patrick Morrissey delivered titles such as "Heaven Knows I'm Miserable Now" (1984) and "Girlfriend in a Coma" (1987) with only the slightest trace of irony.

Morrissey left the band in 1987. With three solo albums behind him (including 1991's *Kill Uncle*), the early nineties find Morrissey poised on the brink of international superstardom. Morrissey is the sensitive man for an apocalyptic decade, a hero for angst-ridden teenagers who would like to laugh at the world, but aren't sure that it's allowed. In the coming decade, one hopes that Morrissey will continue making the world safe for melancholy.

Postpunk

The Smiths were the product of the fabled Manchester scene that also produced Joy Division and New Order. With the success of those groups, Manchester heated up considerably, spawning a raft of bands, mostly dance-oriented, that accompanied massive open-air gatherings at which the highlight was liberal use of the designer drug "ecstasy." Denizens of the revitalized Manchester scene include Jesus Jones, Soup Dragons, EMF, Happy Mondays, and Stone Roses.

Sparked by Down Under's legendary punk outfit, the Saints, Australia's postpunk scene has thrived. From the working-class pubs of Sydney

© Gary Gershoff/Retna Ltd.

comes a no-nonsense brand of rock and roll represented by bands such as Ratcat, the Screaming Jets, Died Pretty, and the Trilobytes. A similar intensity can be heard in the music of Midnight Oil, whose 1987 hit "Beds Are Burning" brought their passionate message of social justice to an international audience.

The postpunk/new-wave boom has also brought international recognition to Australian dance rockers INXS ("Need You Tonight," 1988) and the Hoodoo Gurus, as well as Scotland's Simple Minds ("Don't You Forget About Me," 1985). Meanwhile, New Zealand has fostered wistful postpunk groups the Verlaines, the Clean, the Bats, the Chills, and Straightjacket Fits.

Industrial

Without a doubt, the most potentially radical fallout from the punk explosion is the industrial genre. Responding to the punks' message that humanity had become too degraded to be worth saving, the industrialists raided the technopop camp, pillaging its robotic rhythms and glassy sounds to assemble a chrome-plated monster that walks with a sledgehammer beat and tears through the air like a buzzsaw. Industrial music is punk rock rendered with electronics: relentlessly violent and anguished, but at the same time coldly distanced, as though peering at the world through the digital eye of a computer's image scanner.

Throbbing Gristle and Test Dept. were the seminal industrial aggregations (with a nod toward industrial's art band, Einsturzende Neubauten). Today, the scene writhes with electronic adrenaline, and includes frontrunners Ministry, Foetus, Front 242, the Revolting Cocks, and Front Line Assembly.

The preponderance of great hardcore, postpunk, post-new wave, and industrial bands proves punk's thesis that rock and roll had, indeed, gone stale. Although it was inevitable that punk would self-destruct, it's just as inevitable that the seeds sown during the punk era will continue to nourish the soil of contemporary music for years to come.

Michael Stipe, leader of R.E.M.

The Future of Rock and Roll?

Danger Danger
Giant Sand
Digital Underground
The Troop
Miki Howard
The Rude Boys
En Vogue
After 7
The Manufacturing of Humidifiers
Timmy T
Stevie B
Father M.C.
F.S. Effect
Jasmine Guy
Oleta Adams
Caron Wheeler
Harriet
Londonbeat
Seal
40 Dog
Die Warzau
Alien Sex Fiend
Bitch Magnet
The Blake Babies
3 Mustaphas 3
His Name is Alive
Lush
Bloody Mess
Tim Yohannon
Steel Pole Bathtub
Ace Backwords
Mike Gunderloy
Celtic Frost
Carey Bell
Danielle Dax
The Lemonheads
Bimbox
No External Compulsion
Uncle Smooth
Holocaust
The Buck Pets
The Blanks
Nomeansno
Lard
Springhouse
Sockeye
The Lifers' Group
Sudden Impact
Anacrusis
Sepultura
The Crucified
Mud

Confusion
Fuel
The Offspring
Miss America
The Goober Patrol
Wanton Thought
Sleep
The BBFM's
Bad Religion
Matter of Fact
Mission Impossible
Social Justice
Groundwork
The Bitter End
Morphius
Hullabaloo
Warzone
Chamberphantom
Beyond Sad Weeds
The Eleventh Hour
Every New Dead Ghost
Joy Before the Storm
Bigger Thomas
Bad Trip
Neurosis
The Wrecking Crew
Biohazard
Only Living Witness
Fenton Robinson
Matt Murphy
The Inspiral Carpets
The Attaxe
Jo Jo Anthony
The Weirdos
They Eat Their Own
Guido Toledo
Christian Death
Radio Werewolf
Babes in Toyland
The Heathen
House of Lords
Superchunk
Ward
11th Dream Day
The Common Faces
F/i
Amenity
Born Against
Jane Gulick
The Dambuilders
Big Dipper
Anastasia Screamed

Commission
Suckdog
Marcel Monroe
Jandek
Mitch Landry
Northside
Prisonshake
Buffalo Tom
The Darling Buds
A Guy Called Gerald
Susanna Hoffs
Stormin' Norman
The Anderson Trio
Scat
The Humpers
Christian Lunch
Antietam
Industrial Suicide
The Antisect
Anticimex
The Resistors
Alice in Chains
Redhead Kingpin
Triptich of a Pastel Fern
Poison Gas Research
The Beatnigs
The Dharma Bums
The Aztec Gamers
Romy Haag
The Deep Sea Racing Mullets
Coffin Break
The Skeletons
Mojo Syndrome
Sleep Chamber
Dougzig
Crown of Thorns
Phantasm
White Boy
The Avengers
Leatherface
Radiopuhelimet
The Bones
The Mentors
The Smugglers
The Charlatans
Crime and the City Solution
Whipping Boy
Primal Scream
The Young Gods
Fact 22
KMFDM
Arrhythmia

Birdland
The Ride
Chagall Guevara
Cathy Dennis
The 360's
The Flat Duo Jets
Urge Overkill
The La's
EMF
Xymox
Throwing Muses
Apollo Smile
The Galactic Cowboys
The Candy Skins
I Love You
King of Kings
The Posies
Stan Ridgway
Warrior Soul
Gang Starr
Daniel Ash
The Box
The Cavedogs
Horse
King Tee
Maggie's Dream
School of Fish
Sam Phillips
The Beautiful South
Tragically Hip
Eleventh Dream Day
C + C Music Factory
An Emotional Fish
Morrissey
Fishbone
Happy Mondays
The Screaming Trees
Material Issue
The Heart Throbs
The Goo Goo Dolls
Soho
Gary Stewart
Tricia Leigh Fisher
Jellyfish
Primal Scream
The Sundays
Energy Orchard
The Young Fresh Fellows
David Baerwald
Jimmy Barnes
The Blue Aeroplanes
Maxi Priest

George Makari
The Cows
Bus Driver
Dog Calendar
Colon on the Cob
The Pain Teens
Violent Age
The Bruisers
The Steadies
The Wretched Ones
Czeslaw Nieman
Go!
Makhnovcina
Hollow Heyday
No Security
The Meat Shits
Little Jimmy Dickens
Shooting Star
Amy Pickering
Edgewise
The Toasters
Current 93
The Thrill Kill Kult
Perfect Disaster
Freshly Wrapped Candies
The Melodic Energy
Profax
Man Lifting Banner
Leslie Mackay
Linda Allen
Loup Garou
The Radiators
GG Allin
Jawbox
Dread Zeppelin
More Fiends
Invocator
The Holy Rollers
I Spy
Kelly Willis
The Chicasaw Mudd Puppies
The Lightning Seeds
Bob Mould
Mazzy Star
Kirsty MacColl
Revenge
The Blue Nile
The Chills
Gun
Johnny Clegg

SWEET DREAMS ARE MADE OF THIS:

NEW ROMANTICS AND POP REACTIONARIES

Like the post-hippie apathy that afflicted American rock during the early seventies, a retreat from aggressive posturing and topical lyrics marked the most popular British groups of the postpunk era. Rather than political statements, English youth embraced fashion statements; rather than destroy property, they preferred to dance. One of the more noticeable fashion factions were the new romantics, who dressed up in swashbuckling pirate outfits replete with balloon sleeves, knee-high leather boots, and warpaint-style makeup.

Never one to miss a trend, Malcolm McLaren, former manager of the New York Dolls and the Sex Pistols, assembled the ideal new romantic band. He ended up with two virtually identical units: Adam & the Ants ("Goody Two Shoes," 1982) and Bow Wow Wow ("I Want Candy," 1982), fronted by fetching fourteen-year-old Annabella Lwin. The music was simple and beat-heavy, almost tribal in its dance-obsessed intensity. For a short time, Bow Wow Wow included an effeminate young man named George O'Dowd, known by his friends as Boy George.

A statement in fashion as much as music, Culture Club represented a return to pure pop values after the tumult of punk rock.

Culture Club

George ran a clothing store that was central to the new romantic movement. After Bow Wow Wow, he invented an anti-new-romantic fashion, equally flamboyant but more dandyish, colorful, and fey. Drawing on ex-members of Adam & the Ants and the Clash, he formed Culture Club in 1981, playing a tuneful, soul-inspired pop that bore virtually no relation to the British rock of the previous few years.

Culture Club's first two singles failed to attract any attention, but with the reggae-influenced "Do You Really Want to Hurt Me" in 1982, they had an international hit on their hands. The accompanying album, *Kissing to Be Clever,* was equally strong, but it was Boy George's distinctive persona that attracted the most attention. The band was greeted with headlines such as "Is It A Her? A Him—Or Neither?" Meanwhile, his engaging, witty manner made him a talk-show host's dream. Throughout the next two years, the Club racked up the hits: "I'll Tumble 4 Ya" (1982), "Church of the Poison Mind" (1983), "Karma Chameleon" (1983), "Miss Me Blind" (1984), and others.

By 1985, self-destructive tendencies began to take their toll. When a friend was found dead in Boy George's home, the star's heroin habit became the topic of endless press exposés. But unlike so many rock and roll superstars, George survived, returning as a solo artist in 1987.

Duran Duran

Concurrently with the rise of Culture Club, another new romantic offshoot was making its way across the Atlantic playing lightweight, danceable pop rock. Duran Duran, formed in 1980 "with the idea of crossing Chic with the Sex Pistols," had three minor hits in Britain before breaking worldwide with "Hungry Like the Wolf" in 1982.

One of the first bands to benefit from North American video exposure on MTV and Canada's Much Music, the photogenic quintet found they had to tone down their image in order to be taken seriously. Although critics never succumbed to their charms, they generated an enormous number of international hit singles, including "Is There Something I Should Know" (1983), "The Reflex" (1984), "Wild Boys" (1984), and the James Bond movie theme "View to a Kill" (1985).

In 1985, the group split down the middle, into Arcadia and Power Station (featuring Robert Palmer), each of which made an album before the band regrouped. Meanwhile, guitarist Andy Taylor pursued a solo career, collaborating with ex–Sex Pistol Steve Jones on his first album. He also made cameo appearances on Robert Palmer's "Addicted to Love" and Belinda Carlisle's "Mad About You" (both 1986).

The Eurythmics mined soul, disco, technopop, and pre-British Invasion pop to produce a string of hits throughout the 1980s.

© Syndication International, Ltd.

Pop Reactionaries

The successes of Culture Club and Duran Duran paved the way for a number of talented groups working within the same soul-tinged pop vein. ABC's "Look of Love" (1982) put across a stylish, cosmopolitan image, and Spandau Ballet added synthesizers into the brew on "True" (1983). The Thompson Twins elaborated on Culture Club's approach with "Hold Me Now" (1984). Having captured attention in North America with "People Are People" in 1984, Depeche Mode continued with a string of U.K. hits. Simply Red climbed the charts in 1985 with the soulful "Holding Back the Tears."

In the long term, though, none of the pop reactionaries have been as successful as the Eurythmics.

Eurythmics

Annie Lennox was working as a waitress when she met musician Dave Stewart. Soon they became lovers, but they decided to make music together only after they had broken up. With their first hit, the technodance smash "Sweet Dreams (Are Made of This)" (1983), the Eurythmics looked like another of the technopop duos that flooded England during the late seventies and early eighties.

But the hits kept coming, and the pair's creativity flowered. Lennox, whose outfits ranged from the glamorous to the bizarre, provided a fascinating visual and aural focus, arching between no-holds-barred soul and deadpan new wave. Stewart's songwriting, arranging, and production took the pair through numerous styles, leaving an individual stamp on each. "Here Comes the Rain Again" arrived in 1984, followed by "Would I Lie to You" and "There Must Be an Angel" the next year. In 1985, Lennox teamed up with soul heroine Aretha Franklin for "Sisters Are Doin' It for Themselves."

As of 1991, the Eurythmics are temporarily out of commission, with Stewart having formed his own band, the Spiritual Cowboys. However, the duo's ingenuity and supreme craftsmanship suggest that they'll be back together before long.

Spearheaded by the new romantics, British groups of the early eighties reasserted the value of pure pop after the thrashing it had taken at the hands of the punks. At the same time, they incorporated elements from the best of American and British rock of the previous two decades, updating and elaborating upon them, making them fit for the mercurial musical climate of the nineties.

FEAR OF A BLACK PLANET:
RAP

People sometimes act as if we are making up the stuff we talk about on the records, that we are trying to be controversial and shocking. It is controversial and shocking, but it's also real....Most whites don't know what goes on in this world. They don't even see these streets. The record will be as close as most people get to us.

Ice Cube, 1990

During the mid-fifties, the street corners of Harlem rocked and rolled with the a cappella harmonizing of·African-American musicians too poor to own instruments. Two decades later, the economics of urban culture could provide everyone with at least a turntable. Rather than hire a band, clubs in Harlem and the South Bronx brought in DJs who played the best dance rhythms of the day—an eclectic mix of funk, soul, and hard rock (Queen's funky "Another One Bites the Dust" was a favorite), with an occasional fly ball from left field, maybe the theme song from *The Munsters,* to keep things interesting.

But parties were scarce and DJ hopefuls plentiful. The more competitive contenders began to MC their shows by sending sing-song rhymes out into the audience, exhorting dancers to boogie,

Center: Over funky hip-hop grooves, Public Enemy throws together an intense melange of sampled fragments and black-power rhetoric. Opposite: Run-DMC were the first rappers to qualify for gold, platinum, and finally double-platinum status.

screaming, "wave your hands in the air like you just don't care." MC/DJ teams sprang up overnight; the master of ceremonies rhymed up a storm while the DJ did everything he could to spice up the mix—playing two songs at once on separate turntables, cutting (lifting the needle and backing up the record in a flash to replay a segment of music) and scratching (pulling a disc back and forth across the needle in rhythm). Loud, streetwise, irreverent, and full of good humor, it was grass-roots entertainment at its finest, a new medium created for and by black youth.

The Birth of Rap

The DJ's raps originated in a reggae variation called "toasting," pioneered by the sound system DJs of Jamaica. Indeed, the first New York rapper, DJ Kool Herc, moved to the Bronx from Jamaica when he was twelve years old. Herc presided over the Bronx house party scene in 1975, serving as the center of a clique of DJs that included Afrika Bambaataa, Grandmaster Flash, and Fab 5 Freddie (now MTV's top rap VJ). Rapping belonged exclusively to the South Bronx until Kurtis Blow went public with the first rap record, "Christmas Rappin'," in 1979. Blow's second record, the surprise hit "The Breaks" (1980), sold over a million copies.

Given a public platform, rap entered a period of ferment from which it has yet to chill. With access to album covers, the music developed a visual dimension, mixing and matching Vegas sequins, back-to-Africa dashikis and shell necklaces, B-boy leisure wear such as Kangol caps, sweat suits, and unlaced hi-top sneakers, and ghetto status symbols like gold chains, capped teeth, and enormous nameplate medallions hanging from the neck or worn across four fingers like brass knuckles. Rap allied itself with other forms of black street culture, including the colorful graffitti murals that adorned subway cars and the acrobatics of break dancers spinning on a piece of cardboard for small change. (The term "B-boy," often taken to refer to the residents of the Bronx, originally refered to break dancers.)

Subverting rock and roll's guitar-bass-drums ensemble, the rappers adopted the phonograph and the vinyl disc as their primary accompaniment. The Sugar Hill Gang appropriated Chic's "Good Times" (1979) as the backing track for their own "Rapper's Delight" in 1980, packing an aesthetic, ethical, and legal wallop that still has the industry reeling. The following year, Grandmaster Flash's "Adventures on the Wheels of Steel" showed just what a DJ could do with a pair of turntables. Cutting and scratching with unimaginable virtuosity, Flash's unprecedented aural collage earned critical kudos as "turntable jazz."

the first to appear on Dick Clark's hoary *American Bandstand,* the first on rock-video upstart MTV, and the only rappers to appear at the Live Aid benefit concert. Teaming up with pop-metal has-beens Aerosmith in 1986, Run-DMC revived "Walk This Way," launching Aerosmith on a second career and proving to a skeptical industry, once and for all, that rap and rock belong together.

Rap Gets Seriously Commercial

Run-DMC recorded for the Def Jam label, founded in 1984 by their African-American manager, Russell Simmons, and their white producer, Rick Rubin. Encouraged by Run-DMC's runaway success, Simmons and Rubin realized that what rap was lacking was an Elvis, a white artist capable of performing in the black style without compromising it. If they could find the right gang of white kids, they could open the door for rap to reach the market on a grand scale.

Simmons and Rubin came up with a trio of the most obnoxious middle-class kids they could find. They called them the Beastie Boys. A frat-boy adaptation of Run-DMC's style, the Beasties' first album, *Licensed to Ill* (1986), proved Simmons and Rubin right—to the tune of quadruple platinum. Across North America, white kids raised their fists to the rallying cry, "You've got to fight! For your right! To *paaarty!*"

Rap Gets Serious

Up to that point, rap had been light entertainment, consisting of little more than a clever macho boast over a hip-hop beat. In 1982, Grandmaster Flash and the Furious Five upped the ante with "The Message," a shattering portrayal of ghetto life that chronicled the rise and fall of a black street kid, lamenting "the sad, sad song of how you lived so fast and died so young." "Don't push me, 'cause I'm close to the edge," MC Melle Mel warned, and it was clear that he wasn't just speaking for himself.

Flash and the Five quickly receded into the background with the arrival of Run-DMC. Hailing from middle-class Queens rather than the rundown slums of the Bronx or Harlem, Run-DMC were the stuff of crossover dreams. Rapping in a harsh, declamatory style, they recorded a series of hard-rap hits, beginning with "Rock Box" in 1984, that melded heavy metal riffs with in-your-face ranting. In one fell swoop, they put rap on the commercial map.

By 1986, the Queens posse had become the first rappers to sell gold, platinum, and double-platinum, the first on the cover of *Rolling Stone,*

© Paul Rider/Retna Ltd.

Rap Diversifies

Between Run-DMC and the Beasties, Def Jam created a mass market for rap, and a host of talented young performers stepped up to strut their stuff: LL Cool J, Slick Rick, Doug E. Fresh, Kool Moe Dee, Eric B. & Rakim, Boogie Down Productions, Stetsasonic, Big Daddy Kane, Salt-N-Pepa, and countless others. White rappers also began to proliferate, notably Vanilla Ice and 3rd Bass. Two megapopular rappers, both from Los Angeles, emerged to deepen the genre's commercial potential, Tone-Lōc ("Wild Thing") and Hammer ("U Can't Touch This"). Lōc's 1991 single became the second biggest seller of all time, and Hammer's album *Please Hammer Don't Hurt 'Em* (1990) claimed the Number One spot on Billboard's charts for both pop albums and black albums.

Rap has its antiheroes as well. Public Enemy from New York swept critical polls with *It Takes a Nation of Millions to Hold Us Back* in 1988, an impossibly dense tract of black-power rhetoric and neo-Panther posturing. On the other side of the country, Ice Cube painted hauntingly vivid pictures of gang life in South Central L.A., detailing the savagery of competition both within the community and with local law enforcement. And in Florida, 2 Live Crew tested the limits of free speech (and community tolerance) with near-pornographic lyrics such as "Me So Horny," for which two members of the group were arrested on obscenity charges in 1990.

Once a monolithic expression of disadvantaged youth, rap has fragmented into a legion of subgenres: the neohippie "Afrocentric" wing centered in New York (De La Soul, Queen Latifah, and the Jungle Brothers), big-time pop rap (Hammer,

Tone-Lōc, Vanilla Ice, and New Kids), gangster rap from L.A. (NWA, Ice Cube, and Ice T), and nasty rap (2 Live Crew). The genre's commercial appeal is now unquestionable: Tone-Lōc appears on Pepsi spots, MTV has a regular rap slot (the station's most popular, in fact), and *Newsweek* screamed "Rap Rage!" on its April 1990 cover. And with *The Fresh Prince of Bel Air,* rap has its first bona fide television star. Despite its commercial success, rap was not truly touted by the National Academy of Recording Arts and Sciences until the 1992 Grammy Awards.

It remains to be seen whether rap's vitality can bear up under the weight of such intense hype, exposure, and investment. But there's bound to be a lot of good listening while we're finding out.

Above: Afrocentric rappers De La Soul.

Rock and Roll Children

Jason Bonham (drummer, son of Led Zeppelin's John Bonham)
Debbie Boone (vocalist, daughter of Pat Boone)
Rosanne Cash (vocalist, daughter of Johnny Cash)
Neneh Cherry (vocalist, stepdaughter of jazz trumpeter Don Cherry)
Natalie Cole (vocalist, daughter of Nat "King" Cole)
Sheila E. (drummer, daughter of salsa percussionist Pete Escovedo)
Rockwell (vocalist, son of Motown founder Berry Gordy)
Whitney Houston (vocalist, daughter of gospel singer Cissy Houston)
Julian Lennon (singer/songwriter, son of the late Beatle John Lennon)
Gerald and Sean LeVert (leaders of LeVert, sons of Eddie LeVert of the O'Jays)
Ziggy Marley (vocalist, son of reggae king Bob Marley)
Matthew and Gunnar Nelson (leaders of Nelson, twin sons of the late teen idol Ricky Nelson)
Chynna Phillips (member of Wilson Phillips, daughter of Michelle Phillips of the Mamas & the Papas)
Jeff, Steve, and Mike Porcaro (members of Toto, sons of L.A. session drummer Joe Porcaro)
Zak Starkey (drummer, son of ex-Beatle Ringo Starr)
Carnie and Wendy Wilson (members of Wilson Phillips, daughters of Beach Boy Brian Wilson)
Moon Unit and Dweezil Zappa (daughter and son of Frank Zappa)

Above: Hammer is rap's biggest star yet, having conquered mainstream radio, television, and film. Right: Salt-N-Pepa put a feminine spin on the predominately male rap genre.

GET INTO THE GROOVE:

DISCO REVISIONISM AND HOUSE

The hip-grinding imperative that drove the disco machine burned low during the eighties, when artists from other genres, particularly punk and technopop, dominated the dance floor. But in the nineties, fueled by the kinetic energy of modern rap and funk, dance music is back. What's more, it's back with hooks strong enough to cross over into the pop charts, as demonstrated in 1989 hit singles by Bobby Brown ("Every Little Step"), Jody Watley ("Real Love"), Soul II Soul ("Keep on Movin'"), and former L.A. Laker Girl choreographer Paula Abdul ("Forever Your Girl"), whose debut sold a dizzying 10 million copies by 1991. (Incidentally, Abdul also choreographed Janet Jackson's award-winning video for "Nasty.")

The appeal of a thumping dance beat cuts across racial lines, unifying the faithful of diverse sects. Coupled with a great song, it can cut across other demographic barriers as well, resulting in popularity on a scale that other genres simply can't approach. Anyone who doubts it can cock an ear in the direction of Madonna.

Madonna

Growing up in Michigan with five brothers and two sisters, Madonna Louise Veronica Ciccone was involved in dance, music, and drama throughout her childhood. After a few unsuccessful years in New York as a dancer and actress, she managed to record her first album in 1983, a collection of lightweight pop songs underscored by an unambiguous dance beat.

Meanwhile, Madonna pursued a parallel career as an actress, appearing in several underground films—one of which, *A Certain Sacrifice,* would come back to haunt her when *High Society* magazine excerpted a few frames that showed the singer topless—as well as the features *Vision Quest* and *Desperately Seeking Susan.* First dance clubs and then black radio picked up on three songs from the album, "Holiday," "Borderline," and "Lucky Star." Although *Vision Quest* flopped, *Desperately Seeking Susan* became a surprise box office sensation, and Madonna's career was off to a momentous start.

Critical jibes that her success was a fluke were dashed when *Like a Virgin* hit the stores in 1984. Playing the Madonna/whore dichotomy to the hilt, she stormed the charts with "Like a Virgin," "Material Girl," "Angel," "Into the Groove," and "Dress You Up," the last three of which, in particular, were dance-floor hits. That year Madonna went on tour for the first time, offering the first inkling of her amazing ability to adapt to the whims of the marketplace and to grow as an artist. The 1991 movie *Truth or Dare* documented her extraordinary 1989 stage show and confirmed, once again, the depth of her ambition. Combining a Marilyn Monroe sex-kitten pose with firm control over her own career, Madonna offers a compelling personality, an attractive persona, and increasingly satisfying music.

Madonna, who appeals to blacks and whites, club-goers and stay-at-homes, teeny-boppers and the young at heart, demonstrates the huge market potential of dance music in the era of disco revisionism. But dance clubs also provide fertile ground for local movements, allowing a small community to set itself apart from the mainstream with its own distinct styles of dance, music, dress, and mores. Although some grass-roots movements, such as disco and rap, go national in a big way, others such as Washington, D.C.'s go-go never catch on. In the nineties, the local dance-floor sensation is Chicago's native concoction, house.

Left to right: Paul Abdul, Bobby Brown, Janet Jackson.

House

House music began when Chicago DJs began bringing drum machines and synthesizers into the clubs, using them to beef up the impact of older dance records, as well as to add a personal signature to their shows. Soon, British record companies were hiring them to make dance versions of current hits; a number of the scene's prime movers relocated to England, where the first house records came out during the late eighties. From dance remixes, it was only a short step to eliminating the underlying song entirely, leaving only a sweating, throbbing, danceable core.

In the hands of artists such as D. Mob, A Guy Called Gerald, and Frankie Knuckles, the house sound is similar to vintage disco, but updated and pared down for the age of sensory overload. Gone are the whirling violins and hyped-up romance and/or sexuality; what's left are barebones patterns that vamp endlessly, often without a vocal track—or if there is a vocal, without words. The beat is incessant, mechanical, layered with chattering synthesizers and punctuated by house's trademark piano licks. And, in a variant known as acid house, jarring, unrecognizable sounds scream through the mix, drop-kicking the dance trance into the realm of the surreal.

Paired with full-blown lyrics and melody lines, house has produced a powerful concoction likely to be heard on the dance floor or on the radio. Examples include Deee-lite's "Groove Is in the Heart," (1991); Technotronic's "Pump up the Jam," (1990); and Crystal Waters' "She's Homeless," (1991).

The house scene demonstrates that, in the nineties, the dance club still rivals radio, MTV, and the concert stage as a forum for new talent and stylistic innovation. But it is also a place where disparate styles can meld and merge into the endless beat—something that other ways of presenting music don't seem to be able to achieve. It may be that the crucial musical alliances of the nineties, several of which are already beginning to form, will be forged amidst a mass of writhing, sweating, dancing bodies tuned into a catchy hook and a deep groove.

Madonna has remained on top of the pop charts through the numerous alterations of her image and the increasing sophistication of her music, fashioning herself into the definitive rock star of the 1980s—and perhaps the 1990s as well.

APPETITE FOR DESTRUCTION:

RETRO, SPEED, FUNK, AND DEATH METAL

After lurking in the background for two decades, heavy metal, the misfit geek of rock, has finally asserted its role as one of the dominant forces in modern music. Part and parcel of that dominance has been the fracturing of the metal community along finer stylistic lines to form a plethora of distinctive metal subgenres.

The most popular trend is a throwback to the time when metal was barely distinguishable from hard rock and blues rock: retro metal. Other groups, consolidating the evolution of instrumental virtuosity around metal's tendency toward show-biz acrobatics, play a progressive strain of the music, speed metal. Funk metal also forms its own distinctive enclave, dishing out tasty riffs over nasty, bone-crushing grooves. Metal's most obscure faction is death metal, which fetishizes the demonic imagery that is metal's birthright.

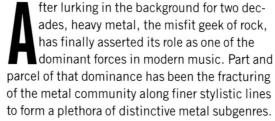

© Eddie Malluk/Retna Ltd.

Retro Metal: Guns N' Roses

One of the most surprising trends of the early nineties is the wholesale appropriation of styles two to three decades old. Groups such as the L.A. Guns and the Black Crowes resurrect the sounds of Aerosmith and the Faces, playing their own compositions as though they were cover versions. Amidst Seattle's teeming club scene, Soundgarden works an intelligent updating of Led Zeppelin. Mudhoney does the same for vintage Black Sabbath, as the Screaming Trees, Nirvana, L7, and the Dwarves follow suit.

So far, the most successful retro metal band has been Guns N' Roses. Although they aren't so apt to wear their influences on their sleeve, GN'R—made up of erstwhile members of the L.A. Guns and Yellow Rose—rocks squarely in the tradition of early seventies hard rock and protometal. Boasting a tough, streetwise image that leans heavily on the pretty-boy swagger of vocalist Axl Rose, they sold 12 million copies of their debut release, *Appetite for Destruction* (1987).

GN'R's enormous success is soured by their glorification of drug addiction and suicide, and more so by the rampant hatemongering of Axl Rose's lyrics in songs such as "One in a Million" (1989). While such sentiments aren't uncommon in heavy metal, GN'R's image isn't tempered by metal's usual cartoonish irony. Nonetheless, the band boasts an exceptional talent in guitarist Slash, and Rose's stage presence is riveting. They opened the nineties with a major tour and an attention-getting dual release, *Use Your Illusion I* and *Use Your Illusion II* (both 1991), and seem destined for continued stardom throughout the decade.

This page: Swaggering pretty-boy Axl Rose fronts the phenomenally successful retro-metal band Guns N' Roses. Opposite: Living Colour crusades for industry acceptance of black rock while playing a muscular brand of funk metal.

Speed Metal

To some extent, metal has always been about chops. It was inevitable that someone would bring the high-powered technique and formal intricacy of progressive rock to the riffing madness of metal.

With their first album, *Master of Puppets* (1986), Metallica did just that. Metallica's music lurches and soars, stops and starts, shifts tempo and meter in an unpredictable frenzy without losing its metal edge. What's more, they don't sing about sex, drugs, or rock and roll. Rather, they vent their frustrations with social conformity, militarism, and censorship. Metallica is the thinking kid's metal band.

Metallica's debut managed to go multiplatinum without the benefit of airplay or video exposure. Dean Mustaine left the group in 1987 to form Megadeth, and since then other speed metal outfits have surfaced, including Anthrax and Slayer. The proliferation of highbrow, supercharged metallurgists considerably broadens metal's scope, upping the ante for the music's importance in the nineties.

Funk Metal

African-American musicians have played a crucial role at virtually every stage of rock and roll history, from Chuck Berry to Hendrix to Sly to Bob Marley to Poly Styrene, the pudgy lead vocalist for U.K. punk pioneers X-Ray Spex. Nonetheless, black and white players tend to divide along stylistic boundaries. Metal has remained 100 percent white.

That is, until now. Spearheaded by Vernon Reid's Black Rock Coalition, a movement is gathering that promises to make black musicianship a permanent part of the rock mainstream, rather than relegated to traditionally black styles such as soul and funk. Black rock and roll bands such as Fishbone, who toss in a dollop of ironic humor, as

well as white groups including Faith No More and the Red Hot Chili Peppers, herald a fusion of metal and funk that borders on the revolutionary.

The premier funk-metal band is Vernon Reid's own group, Living Colour. Beginning with *Vivid* in 1988, Living Colour has been laying down slammin' grooves that crunch, throb, and wail with Reid's formidable guitar prowess while speaking eloquently about the challenges of modern society. The group supported the Rolling Stones on their 1989 Steel Wheels Tour, returning to an avalanche of awards, critical raves, and reader-poll recognition. With the Grammy-winning *Time's Up* (1990), they entered the new decade fully prepared to erase rock and roll's racial boundaries once and for all.

Death Metal

Conjuring arcane satanic rituals, the death metallers remain deliberately obscure. They trade in the same ethos of evil that, say, Motley Crüe does, but with a harrowing difference: They appear to mean it. Groups with names such as Mordred, Kreator, Sepultura, Anacrusis, and Godflesh wallow in the prospect of human sacrifice, burning flesh, dismemberment, torture, and the erotic implications thereof. Unlikely to gain a following of much size, death metal nonetheless challenges the norms of taste in a way that the best rock and roll always has. And produces terrifying videos, to boot.

EPILOGUE

Dancing on the threshold of the millennium, rock and roll struts its stuff in a vertiginous pageant of musical, visual, and philosophical styles. While fashions come and go at a dizzying pace, the music seems to gain by what has come before, rather than discarding the past altogether in its headlong drive toward the future. Up-to-the-minute freshness may be part and parcel of the current landscape, but time-honored rock and roll traditions abound, anchored in the archetypal images of the visionary troubadour, the hard-working, hard-playing band, and the overt phallic symbolism of the electric guitar.

One tradition that is firmly established is rock and roll's unholy alliance with big business. Ever since the days of white remakes of R&B hits, the majors—virtually all of which are now owned by multinational corporations—have called the shots, buying up the most popular acts and manipulating the trends. Only during the punk era did small labels threaten to upset the hegemony of the majors. But they proved capable of holding their own, and today the indies serve only as proving ground for young bands and new styles. As soon as anything shows commercial potential, the majors snap it up.

The inevitable progeny of rock and roll's marriage of art and commerce are manufactured stars such as the Monkees and New Kids on the Block. Milli Vanilli caused a stir in 1990 by winning a Grammy (later rescinded) on the strength of vocals that turned out to have been performed by a hired hand. In fact, Milli Vanilli's methods were only part of a tradition that stretches decades into the past. That wasn't Ringo slamming the skins on the Beatles' first single. Likewise, Tina Weymouth didn't play bass on much of the first Talking Heads album.

Despite the industry's feigned outrage over the incident, the Milli Vanilli affair didn't herald the decline of Western civilization. "Product" has often been among the best music in the Top Ten—during the sixties, no lesser an authority than Frank Zappa championed the Monkees—and, in any case, where

rock and roll is concerned, the line between manipulation and inspiration is a thin one. If nothing else, Milli Vanilli suggests a split between stars who record and those who perform. The majors' tight control over record promotion and distribution may well force some bands to develop a reputation solely as concert artists, while the charts continue to fill up with recording artists who wouldn't be capable of working a live audience (and who, in fact, may be nothing more than a computer-generated doppelganger in the mold of Max Headroom). Eventually, great performers may be accorded the same status as major recording stars, even though they don't make records.

The abstraction of rock and roll from live performance, which began with multitrack recording during the early sixties, became more or less complete with the advent of MTV in 1981. Bands that didn't have a prayer of making it through a concert could be fully convincing on videotape. As an audiovisual medium, rock video raised the music's visual aspect onto equal footing with the sound itself. The impact was immediate, as hair and clothing styles, facial expressions, and body postures became ever more mannered. The abortive innovations of seventies-style glitter rockers such as David Bowie and Alice Cooper offer a blueprint for much of what the video future might bring.

The intensely visual focus of music video has also brought rock's color barriers into sharp relief. Although the late eighties and early nineties have been relatively apolitical in terms of popular culture, race relations have become a central issue in rock and roll. Spurred by rap's insistence on black identity and social relevance, rock has become a laboratory for exploring ways in which the boundary between black and white might be erased, and music video offers a space in which black and white artists can interact to dramatic effect. At the same time, television channels such as MTV and Much Music offer opportunities to experiment with programming formats that radio has ignored since the seventies. The moguls of broadcasting are finding that there's more money in mixing black and white music, thereby blurring the distinction between the two and contributing to one of the most exciting cultural developments in years.

Similar things are happening on an international scale. The popular music of cultures outside North America and Europe was once regarded as appealing only to local audiences. As the eighties began, increased immigration, the success of reggae, and the record industry's insatiable attraction to novelty began to boost records from other nations into the charts. Meanwhile, stars from South America, Africa, the Middle East, and elsewhere have toured in the West, developing enthusiastic followings and bringing new sounds into the palette of mainstream rock. "World Beat" scenes have sprung up in cities such as San Francisco and London as rock and rollers apply exotic licks and rhythms to their own music. The process, initiated by Paul Simon (Graceland) and Talking Heads (Naked), is only beginning. In coming years, North American and British hits will routinely boast influences from around the world.

Of course, the driving force behind such sweeping changes is technology—the technology of recording production and distribution. New technology influences music more directly as well, with new instruments like drum machines and synthesizers spawning substyles such as house and cyberpunk. Sampling—which makes it possible to record snippets of records for playback from a keyboard—is now endemic in rap, and forces a reexamination of everything from the aesthetics of songwriting to copyright law. The technique of collage, long a staple of the visual arts, is now a viable way of rocking out. Sampling artists take the best of the old and weave it into something new, pushing musical creativity in directions undreamed of only a short time ago.

That so many possibilities still exist for rock and roll is an indication of the music's tremendous vigor and stamina. In thirty-five years—enough, in a bygone era, to render even the most reliable person untrustworthy—rock has been born, grown old, and been born again several times over. With each lifetime, it grows in scope and blazes new pathways toward a more all-encompassing form of expression. "Long live rock, be it dead or alive," Pete Townshend sang, but indeed, rock and roll is thirty-five years young—still brash, loud, stuttering, and absurdly confident that, against all odds, it can bring to modern culture the salvation that it so badly needs. So far, it's been an amazing ride. Here's to another thirty-five years.

Grammy Awards

1958
Record of the Year: "Volare (Nel Blu Dipinto Di Blu)," Domenico Modugno
Song of the Year: "Volare (Nel Blu Dipinto Di Blu)," words and music by Domenico Modugno
Album of the Year: *The Music From Peter Gunn,* Henry Mancini
Best Vocal, Female: *Ella Fitzgerald Sings the Irving Berlin Songbook*
Best Vocal, Male: "Catch a Falling Star," Perry Como
Best Vocal, Group: "That Old Black Magic," Louis Prima & Keely Smith

1959
Record of the Year: "Mack the Knife," Bobby Darin
Song of the Year: "The Battle of New Orleans," words and music by Jimmy Driftwood
Album of the Year: *Come Dance With Me,* Frank Sinatra
Best Vocal, Female: "But Not For Me," Ella Fitzgerald
Best Vocal, Male: *Come Dance With Me,* Frank Sinatra
Best New Artist: Bobby Darin

1960
Record of the Year: "Theme From *A Summer Place,*" Percy Faith
Song of the Year: "Theme From *Exodus,*" words and music by Ernest Gold
Album of the Year: *The Button-Down Mind of Bob Newhart*
Best Vocal, Female: "Mack the Knife," Ella Fitzgerald
Best Vocal, Male: "Georgia on My Mind," Ray Charles
Best Vocal, Group: *We Got Us,* Steve Lawrence & Eydie Gorme
Best New Artist: Bob Newhart

1961
Record of the Year: "Moon River," Henry Mancini
Song of the Year: "Moon River," words by Johnny Mercer, music by Henry Mancini
Album of the Year: *Judy at Carnegie Hall,* Judy Garland
Best Vocal, Female: *Judy at Carnegie Hall,* Judy Garland
Best Vocal, Male: "Lollipops and Roses," Jack Jones
Best Vocal, Group: "High Flying," Lambert, Hendricks & Ross
Best Rock and Roll Recording: "Let's Twist Again," Chubby Checker
Best New Artist: Peter Nero

1962
Record of the Year: "I Left My Heart in San Francisco," Tony Bennett
Song of the Year: "What Kind of a Fool Am I," words by Anthony Newley, music by Leslie Bricusse
Album of the Year: *The First Family,* Vaughn Meader
Best Vocal, Female: *Ella Fitzgerald Swings With Nelson Riddle*
Best Vocal, Male: *I Left My Heart in San Francisco,* Tony Bennett
Best Vocal, Group: "If I Had a Hammer," Peter, Paul & Mary
Best Rock and Roll Recording: "Alley Cat," Bent Fabric
Best New Artist: Robert Goulet

1963
Record of the Year: "Days of Wine and Roses," Henry Mancini
Song of the Year: "Days of Wine and Roses," words by Johnny Mercer, music by Henry Mancini
Album of the Year: *The Barbra Streisand Album*
Best Vocal, Female: *The Barbra Streisand Album*
Best Vocal, Male: "Wives and Lovers," Jack Jones
Best Vocal, Group: "Blowin' in the Wind," Peter, Paul & Mary
Best Rock and Roll Recording: "Deep Purple," Nino Tempo & April Stevens
Best New Artist: the Swingle Singers

1964
Record of the Year: "The Girl From Ipanema," Stan Getz & Astrud Gilberto
Song of the Year: "Hello, Dolly!" words and music by Jerry Herman
Album of the Year: *Getz/Gilberto,* Stan Getz & Astrud Gilberto
Best Vocal, Female: "People," Barbra Streisand
Best Vocal, Male: "Hello, Dolly!" Louis Armstrong
Best Vocal, Group: "A Hard Day's Night," the Beatles
Best Rock and Roll Recording: "Downtown," Petula Clark
Best New Artist: the Beatles

1965
Record of the Year: "A Taste of Honey," Herb Alpert & the Tijuana Brass
Song of the Year: "The Shadow of Your Smile," words by Paul Francis Webster, music by Johnny Mandel
Album of the Year: *September of My Years,* Frank Sinatra
Best Vocal, Female: *My Name is Barbra,* Barbra Streisand
Best Vocal, Male: "It Was a Very Good Year," Frank Sinatra
Best Vocal, Group: *We Dig Mancini,* the Anita Kerr Singers
Best Rock and Roll Single: "King of the Road," Roger Miller
Best New Artist: Tom Jones

1966
Record of the Year: "Strangers in the Night," Frank Sinatra
Song of the Year: "Michelle," words and music by John Lennon & Paul McCartney
Album of the Year: *Sinatra: A Man and His Music,* Frank Sinatra
Best Vocal, Female: "If He Walked Into My Life," Eydie Gorme
Best Vocal, Male: "Strangers in the Night," Frank Sinatra
Best Vocal, Group: "A Man and a Woman," the Anita Kerr Singers
Best Rock and Roll Recording: "Winchester Cathedral," the New Vaudeville Band

1967
Record of the Year: "Up, Up and Away," the 5th Dimension
Song of the Year: "Up, Up and Away," words and music by Jim Webb
Album of the Year: *Sgt. Pepper's Lonely Hearts Club Band,* the Beatles
Best Vocal, Female: "Ode to Billie Joe," Bobbie Gentry
Best Vocal, Male: "By the Time I Get to Phoenix," Glen Campbell
Best Vocal, Group: "Up, Up and Away," the 5th Dimension
Best Contemporary Single: "Up, Up and Away," the 5th Dimension
Best New Artist: Bobbie Gentry

1968
Record of the Year: "Mrs. Robinson," Simon & Garfunkel
Song of the Year: "Little Green Apples," words and music by Bobby Russell
Album of the Year: *By the Time I Get to Phoenix,* Glen Campbell
Best Contemporary/Pop Vocal, Female: "Do You Know the Way to San Jose," Dionne Warwick
Best Contemporary/Pop Vocal, Male: "Light My Fire," Jose Feliciano
Best Contemporary/Pop Vocal, Group: "Mrs. Robinson," Simon & Garfunkel
Best New Artist: Jose Feliciano

1969
Record of the Year: "Aquarius/Let the Sun Shine In," the 5th Dimension
Song of the Year: "Games People Play," words and music by Joe South
Album of the Year: *Blood, Sweat & Tears*
Best Contemporary Vocal, Female: "Is That All There Is," Peggy Lee
Best Contemporary Vocal, Male: "Everybody's Talkin'," Harry Nilsson
Best Contemporary Vocal, Group: "Aquarius/Let the Sun Shine In," the 5th Dimension
Best New Artist: Crosby, Stills & Nash

1970
Record of the Year: "Bridge Over Troubled Water," Simon & Garfunkel
Song of the Year: "Bridge Over Troubled Water," words and music by Paul Simon
Album of the Year: *Bridge Over Troubled Water,* Simon & Garfunkel
Best Contemporary Vocal, Female: *I'll Never Fall in Love Again,* Dionne Warwick
Best Contemporary Vocal, Male: "Everything Is Beautiful," Ray Stevens
Best Contemporary Vocal, Group: "(They Long to Be) Close to You," the Carpenters
Best New Artist: the Carpenters

1971
Record of the Year: "It's Too Late," Carole King
Song of the Year: "You've Got a Friend," words and music by Carole King
Album of the Year: *Tapestry,* Carole King
Best Contemporary Vocal, Female: *Tapestry,* Carole King
Best Contemporary Vocal, Male: "You've Got a Friend," James Taylor
Best Contemporary Vocal, Group: *The Carpenters*
Best New Artist: Carly Simon

1972
Record of the Year: "The First Time Ever I Saw Your Face," Roberta Flack
Song of the Year: "The First Time Ever I Saw Your Face," words and music by Ewan MacColl
Album of the Year: *The Concert for Bangladesh,* George Harrison & Friends
Best Pop Vocal, Female: "I Am Woman," Helen Reddy
Best Pop Vocal, Male: "Without You," Nilsson
Best Pop Vocal, Group: "Where Is the Love," Roberta Flack & Donny Hathaway
Best New Artist: America

1973
Record of the Year: "Killing Me Softly With His Song," Roberta Flack
Song of the Year: "Killing Me Softly With His Song," words by Norman Gimbel, music by Charles Fox
Album of the Year: *Innervisions,* Stevie Wonder
Best Pop Vocal, Female: "Killing Me Softly With His Song," Roberta Flack
Best Pop Vocal, Male: "You Are the Sunshine of My Life," Stevie Wonder
Best Pop Vocal, Group: "Neither One Of Us (Wants to Be the First to Say Goodbye)," Gladys Knight & the Pips
Best New Artist: Bette Midler

1974
Record of the Year: "I Honestly Love You," Olivia Newton-John
Song of the Year: "The Way We Were," words by Alan & Marilyn Bergman, music by Marvin Hamlisch
Album of the Year: *Fulfillingness' First Finale,* Stevie Wonder
Best Pop Vocal, Female: "I Honestly Love You," Olivia Newton-John
Best Pop Vocal, Male: *Fulfillingness' First Finale,* Stevie Wonder
Best Pop Vocal, Group: "Band on the Run," Paul McCartney & Wings
Best New Artist: Marvin Hamlisch

1975
Record of the Year: "Love Will Keep Us Together," the Captain & Tenille
Song of the Year: "Send in the Clowns," words and music by Stephen Sondheim
Album of the Year: *Still Crazy After All These Years,* Paul Simon
Best Pop Vocal, Female: "At Seventeen," Janis Ian
Best Pop Vocal, Male: *Still Crazy After All These Years,* Paul Simon
Best Pop Vocal, Group: "Lyin' Eyes," the Eagles
Best New Artist: Natalie Cole

1976
Record of the Year: "This Masquerade," George Benson
Song of the Year: "I Write the Songs," Bruce Johnston
Album of the Year: *Songs in the Key of Life,* Stevie Wonder
Best Pop Vocal, Female: *Hasten Down the Wind,* Linda Ronstadt
Best Pop Vocal, Male: *Songs in the Key of Life,* Stevie Wonder
Best Pop Vocal, Group: "If You Leave Me Now," Chicago
Best New Artist: the Starland Vocal Band

1977
Record of the Year: "Hotel California," the Eagles
Song of the Year: "Love Theme From *A Star Is Born* (Evergreen)," words by Paul Williams, music by Barbra Streisand; "You Light Up My Life," words and music by Joe Brooks
Album of the Year: *Rumours,* Fleetwood Mac
Best Pop Vocal, Female: "Love Theme From *A Star Is Born* (Evergreen)," Barbra Streisand
Best Pop Vocal, Male: "Handy Man," James Taylor
Best Pop Vocal, Group: "How Deep Is Your Love," the Bee Gees
Best New Artist: Debby Boone

1978
Record of the Year: "Just the Way You Are," Billy Joel
Song of the Year: "Just the Way You Are," words and music by Billy Joel
Album of the Year: *Saturday Night Fever,* the Bee Gees, David Shire, Yvonne Elliman, Tavares, Kool & the Gang, K.C. & the Sunshine Band, MFSB, the Trammps, Walter Murphy, Ralph McDonald
Best Pop Vocal, Female: "You Needed Me," Anne Murray
Best Pop Vocal, Male: "Copacabana," Barry Manilow
Best Pop Vocal, Group: "Night Fever," the Bee Gees
Best New Artist: A Taste of Honey

1979
Record of the Year: "What a Fool Believes," the Doobie Brothers
Song of the Year: "What a Fool Believes," words and music by Kenny Loggins & Michael McDonald
Album of the Year: *52nd Street,* Billy Joel
Best Vocal, Female: "I'll Never Love This Way Again," Dionne Warwick
Best Vocal, Male: *52nd Street,* Billy Joel
Best Vocal, Group: "Minute by Minute," the Doobie Brothers
Best Rock Vocal, Female: "Hot Stuff," Donna Summer
Best Rock Vocal, Male: "Gotta Serve Somebody," Bob Dylan
Best Rock Vocal, Group: "Heartache Tonight," the Eagles
Best New Artist: Rickie Lee Jones

1980
Record of the Year: "Sailing," Christopher Cross
Song of the Year: "Sailing," words and music by Christopher Cross
Album of the Year: *Christopher Cross*
Best Vocal, Female: "The Rose," Bette Midler
Best Vocal, Male: "This Is It," Kenny Loggins
Best Vocal, Group: "Guilty," Barbra Streisand & Barry Gibb
Best Rock Vocal, Female: *Crimes of Passion,* Pat Benatar
Best Rock Vocal, Male: *Glass Houses,* Billy Joel
Best Rock Vocal, Group: *Against the Wind,* Bob Seger & the Silver Bullet Band
Best New Artist: Christopher Cross

1981
Record of the Year: "Bette Davis Eyes," Kim Carnes
Song of the Year: "Bette Davis Eyes," words and music by Donna Weiss & Jackie De Shannon
Album of the Year: *Double Fantasy,* John Lennon & Yoko Ono
Best Vocal, Female: *Lena Horne: The Lady and Her Music*
Best Vocal, Male: Breakin' Away, Al Jarreau
Best Vocal, Group: "Boy From New York City," the Manhattan Transfer
Best Rock Vocal, Female: "Fire and Ice," Pat Benatar
Best Rock Vocal, Male: "Jessie's Girl," Rick Springfield
Best Rock Vocal, Group: "Don't Stand So Close to Me," the Police
Best New Artist: Sheena Easton

1982
Record of the Year: "Rosanna," Toto
Song of the Year: "Always on My Mind," words and music by Johnny Christopher, Mark James & Wayne Carson
Album of the Year: *Toto IV*
Best Vocal, Female: "You Should Hear How She Talks About You," Melissa Manchester
Best Vocal, Male: "Truly," Lionel Richie
Best Vocal, Group: "Up Where We Belong," Joe Cocker & Jennifer Warnes
Best Rock Vocal, Female: "Shadows of the Night," Pat Benatar
Best Rock Vocal, Male: "Hurts So Good," John Cougar
Best Rock Vocal, Group: "Eye of the Tiger," Survivor
Best New Artist: Men at Work

1983
Record of the Year: "Beat It," Michael Jackson
Song of the Year: "Every Breath You Take," words and music by Sting
Album of the Year: *Thriller,* Michael Jackson
Best Vocal, Female: "Flashdance…What a Feeling," Irene Cara
Best Vocal, Male: *Thriller,* Michael Jackson
Best Vocal, Group: "Every Breath You Take," the Police
Best Rock Vocal, Female: "Love Is a Battlefield," Pat Benatar
Best Rock Vocal, Male: "Beat It," Michael Jackson
Best Rock Vocal, Group: *Synchronicity,* the Police
Best New Artist: Culture Club

1984
Record of the Year: "What's Love Got to Do With It," Tina Turner
Song of the Year: "What's Love Got to Do With It," words and music by Graham Lyle & Terry Britten
Album of the Year: *Can't Slow Down,* Lionel Richie
Best Vocal, Female: "What's Love Got to Do With It," Tina Turner
Best Vocal, Male: "Against All Odds (Take a Look at Me Now)," Phil Collins
Best Vocal, Group: "Jump (for My Love)," the Pointer Sisters
Best Rock Vocal, Female: "Better Be Good to Me," Tina Turner
Best Rock Vocal, Male: "Dancing in the Dark," Bruce Springsteen
Best Rock Vocal, Group: *Purple Rain,* Prince & the Revolution
Best New Artist: Cyndi Lauper

1985
Record of the Year: "We Are the World," USA for Africa
Song of the Year: "We Are the World," words and music by Michael Jackson & Lionel Richie
Album of the Year: *No Jacket Required,* Phil Collins
Best Vocal, Female: "Saving All My Love for You," Whitney Houston
Best Vocal, Male: *No Jacket Required,* Phil Collins
Best Vocal, Group: "We Are the World," USA for Africa
Best Rock Vocal, Female: "One of the Living," Tina Turner
Best Rock Vocal, Male: "The Boys of Summer," Don Henley
Best Rock Vocal, Group: "Money for Nothing," Dire Straits
Best New Artist: Sade

1986
Record of the Year: "Higher Love," Steve Winwood
Song of the Year: "That's What Friends Are for," words and music by Burt Bacharach & Carol Bayer Sager
Album of the Year: *Graceland,* Paul Simon
Best Vocal, Female: *The Broadway Album,* Barbra Streisand
Best Vocal, Male: "Higher Love," Steve Winwood
Best Vocal, Group: "That's What Friends Are for," Dionne Warwick, Stevie Wonder, Elton John & Gladys Knight
Best Rock Vocal, Female: *Break Every Rule,* Tina Turner
Best Rock Vocal, Male: "Addicted to Love," Robert Palmer
Best Rock Vocal, Group: "Missionary Man," Eurythmics
Best New Artist: Bruce Hornsby & the Range

1987
Record of the Year: "Graceland," Paul Simon
Song of the Year: "Somewhere Out There," words and music by James Horner, Barry Mann & Cynthia Weil
Album of the Year: *The Joshua Tree,* U2
Best Pop Vocal, Female: "I Wanna Dance With Somebody (Who Loves Me), Whitney Houston
Best Pop Vocal, Male: *Bring on the Night,* Sting
Best Pop Vocal, Group: "(I've Had) The Time of My Life," Bill Medley & Jennifer Warnes
Best Pop Instrumental: "Minute by Minute," Larry Carlton
Best Rock Vocal, Female or Male: "Tunnel of Love," Bruce Springsteen
Best Rock Vocal, Group: *The Joshua Tree,* U2
Best Rock Instrumental: "Jazz From Hell," Frank Zappa
Best R&B Performance, Female: *Aretha,* Aretha Franklin
Best R&B Performance, Male: "Just to See Her," Smokey Robinson
Best R&B Performance, Group: "I Knew You Were Waiting (for Me)," Aretha Franklin & George Michael
Best R&B Instrumental: "Chicago Song," David Sanborn
Best R&B Song: "Lean on Me," words and music by Bill Withers
Best New Artist: Jody Watley

1988
Record of the Year: "Don't Worry, Be Happy," Bobby McFerrin
Song of the Year: "Don't Worry, Be Happy," words and music by Bobby McFerrin
Album of the Year: *Faith,* George Michael
Best Pop Vocal, Female: "Fast Car," Tracy Chapman
Best Pop Vocal, Male: "Don't Worry, Be Happy," Bobby McFerrin
Best Pop Vocal, Group: "Brazil," the Manhattan Transfer
Best Pop Instrumental: "Close Up," David Sanborn
Best Rock Vocal, Female: *Tina Live in Europe,* Tina Turner
Best Rock Vocal, Male: "Simply Irresistible," Robert Palmer
Best Rock Vocal, Group: "Desire," U2
Best Rock Instrumental: "Blues for Salvadore," Carlos Santana
Best Hard Rock/Metal Performance: *Crest of a Knave,* Jethro Tull
Best R&B Performance, Female: "Giving You the Best That I Got," Anita Baker
Best R&B Performance, Male: *Introducing the Hardline According to Terence Trent D'Arby,* Terence Trent D'Arby
Best R&B Performance, Group: "Love Overboard," Gladys Knight & the Pips
Best R&B Instrumental: *Light Years,* Chick Corea
Best R&B Song: "Giving You the Best That I Got," Anita Baker
Best Rap Performance: "Parents Just Don't Understand," DJ Jazzy Jeff & the Fresh Prince
Best Video: "Where the Streets Have No Name," U2
Best New Artist: Tracy Chapman

1989
Record of the Year: "Wind Beneath My Wings," Bette Midler
Song of the Year: "Wind Beneath My Wings," Bette Midler
Album of the Year: *Nick of Time,* Bonnie Raitt
Best Pop Vocal, Female: "Nick of Time," Bonnie Raitt
Best Pop Vocal, Male: "How Am I Supposed to Live Without You," Michael Bolton
Best Pop Vocal, Group: "Don't Know Much," Linda Ronstadt & Aaron Neville
Best Pop Instrumental: "Healing Chant," the Neville Brothers
Best Rock Vocal, Female: *Nick of Time,* Bonnie Raitt
Best Rock Vocal, Male: *The End of the Innocence,* Don Henley
Best Rock Vocal, Group: *Traveling Wilburys Volume One*
Best Rock Instrumental: *Jeff Beck's Guitar Shop with Terry Bozio and Tony Hymas*
Best Hard Rock Performance: "Cult of Personality," Living Colour
Best Metal Performance: "One," Metallica
Best R&B Vocal, Female: *Giving You the Best That I Got,* Anita Baker
Best R&B Vocal, Male: "Every Little Step," Bobby Brown
Best R&B Vocal, Group: "Back to Life," Soul II Soul
Best R&B Instrumental: "African Dance," Soul II Soul
Best R&B Song: "If You Don't Know Me By Now," Simply Red
Best Rap Performance: "Bust a Move," Young MC
Best Contemporary Blues Recording: *In Step,* Stevie Ray Vaughan & Double Trouble
Best Contemporary Folk Recording: *Indigo Girls*
Best Reggae Recording: *One Bright Day,* Ziggy Marley & the Melody Makers
Best Jazz Fusion Performance: *Letter From Home,* Pat Metheny Group
Best Video, Short Form: "Leave Me Alone," Michael Jackson
Best Video, Long Form: *Rhythm Nation 1814,* Janet Jackson

1990
Record of the Year: "Another Day in Paradise," Phil Collins
Song of the Year: "From a Distance," words and music by Julie Gold
Album of the Year: *Back on the Block,* Quincy Jones
Best Pop Vocal, Female: "Vision of Love," Mariah Carey
Best Pop Vocal, Male: "Oh Pretty Woman," Roy Orbison
Best Pop Vocal, Group: "All My Life," Linda Ronstadt & Aaron Neville
Best Pop Instrumental: "Twin Peaks" Theme," Angelo Badalamenti
Best Rock Vocal, Female: "Black Velvet," Alannah Myles
Best Rock Vocal, Male: "Bad Love," Eric Clapton
Best Rock Vocal, Group: "Janie's Got a Gun," Aerosmith
Best Rock Instrumental: "D/FW," the Vaughan Brothers
Best Hard Rock Performance: *Time's Up,* Living Colour
Best Metal Performance: "Stone Cold Crazy," Metallica
Best Alternative Music Performance: *I Do Not Want What I Haven't Got,* Sinead O'Connor

1989 (continued)
Best R&B Vocal, Female: *Compositions,* Anita Baker
Best R&B Vocal, Male: "Here and Now," Luther Vandross
Best R&B Vocal, Group: "I'll Be Good to You," Ray Charles & Chaka Khan
Best R&B Song: "U Can't Touch This," words and music by Rick James, Alonzo Miller & M.C. Hammer
Best Rap, Solo: "U Can't Touch This," M.C. Hammer
Best Rap, Group: "Back on the Block," Quincy Jones (featuring Ice-T, Melle Mel, Big Daddy Kane, Kool Moe Dee, and Quincy D. III)
Best Contemporary Blues Recording: *Family Style,* the Vaughan Brothers
Best Contemporary Folk Recording: *Steady on,* Shawn Colvin
Best Reggae Recording: *Time Will Tell: A Tribute to Bob Marley,* Bunny Wailer
Best Jazz Fusion Performance: "Birdland," Quincy Jones
Best Rock/Contemporary Gospel Album: *Beyond Belief,* Petra
Best Video, Short Form: "Opposites Attract," Paula Abdul
Best Video, Long Form: *Please Hammer Don't Hurt 'Em,* M.C. Hammer
Best New Artist: Mariah Carey

1991
Record of the Year: "Unforgettable," Natalie Cole
Song of the Year: "Unforgettable," words and music by Irving Gordon
Album of the Year: *Unforgettable,* Natalie Cole
Best Pop Vocal, Female: "Something to Talk About," Bonnie Raitt
Best Pop Vocal, Male: "When a Man Loves a Woman," Michael Bolton
Best Pop Vocal, Group: "Unforgettable," Natalie Cole with Nat (King) Cole
Best Pop Instrumental: *Robin Hood: Prince of Thieves,* Michael Kamen conducting the greater Los Angeles Orchestra
Best Rock Vocal, Solo: *Luck of the Draw,* Bonnie Raitt
Best Rock Vocal, Group: "Good Man, Good Woman," Bonnie Raitt and Delbert McClinton
Best Rock Instrumental: "Cliffs of Dover," Eric Johnson
Best Rock Song: "The Soul Cages," Sting
Best Hard Rock Performance: *For Unlawful Carnal Knowledge,* Van Halen
Best Metal Performance: *Metallica,* Metallica
Best Alternative Performance: *Out of Time,* R.E.M.
Best R&B Vocal, Female: Patti LaBelle *(Burnin')* and Lisa Fischer *(So Intense)* (tie)
Best R&B Vocal, Male: Luther Vandross, *Power of Love*
Best R&B Vocal, Group: Boyz II Men, *Cooleyhighharmony*
Best R&B Song: "Power of Love/Love Power," Luther Vandross, Marcus Miller & Teddy Vann
Best Rap, Solo: "Mama Said Knock You Out," LL Cool J
Best Rap, Group: "Summertime," D.J. Jazzy Jeff and the Fresh Prince
Best Contemporary Blues Recording: "Damn Right I've Got the Blues," Buddy Guy
Best Contemporary Folk Recording: John Prine, *The Missing Years*
Best Reggae Recording: "As Raw as Ever," Shabba Ranks
Best Contemporary Jazz Performance: "Sassy," The Manhattan Transfer
Best Rock Contemporary Gospel Album: *Under Their Influence,* Russ Taff
Best Video, Short Form: "Losing My Religion," R.E.M.
Best Video, Long Form: *Blonde Ambition World Tour Live,* Madonna
Best New Artist: Marc Cohn